Don't "Should" On Your Kids

Build their mental toughness

D0339252

Dr. Rob Bell & Bill Parisi

ISBN 978-0-9899184-1-1 (Hardback)
ISBN 978-0-9899184-2-8 (Paperback)
ISBN 978-0-9899184-3-5 (E-book)

Book Design: Fresh Design, Inc.

Published by
DRB Press

ALSO BY DR. ROB BELL

Mental Toughness Training for Golf

The Hinge: The Importance of Mental Toughness

NO FEAR: A Simple Guide to Mental Toughness

Follow *Don't Should on Your Kids* at

 The-Hinge-The-Importance-of-Mental-Toughness

 @parisispeed   www.parisischool.com
@drrobbell   www.drrobbell.com
#DontShould

Advance Praise

"As a NFL head coach, when a bad play occurs, we need to move on and focus on the next one. As parents, the best focus means enjoying the process of our kids' journey and being supportive along the way. This book helps with our kids and our own mental toughness."

— CHUCK PAGANO, NFL HEAD COACH

"Read this book and I'll send you a participation trophy."

— JOHN BRUBAKER, AWARD-WINNING AUTHOR, COACH & PARENT

"Just like in **The Hinge**, this book provides both parents and coaches with simple, actionable steps to help their athletes develop mental toughness. I highly recommend it."

— JOHN O'SULLIVAN, AUTHOR OF **CHANGING THE GAME**.

"Rob Bell and Bill Parisi have contributed an important distinction between 'supportive parents and vicarious parents.' Don't Should on Your Kids includes many practical thoughts for parents including one of my favorites, 'Great parents ask their kid, How was your day?' not just 'How was your practice?'"

— JIM THOMPSON, POSITIVE COACHING ALLIANCE FOUNDER AND AUTHOR OF **ELEVATING YOUR GAME: BECOMING A TRIPLE-IMPACT COMPETITOR**

The Contributors

Thank you to the 105 coaches, parents and leaders who contributed to this book.

Contributor	Website
Adam Ritz	www.adamritz.com
Adam Schaechterle	www.und.com
Adam Spencer	
Adam Wiginton	www.twitter.com/coachwig
Alan Edwards	www.lamarcardinals.com
Alan Jaeger	www.jaegersports.com
Alexa Dvorak	www.twitter.com/alexajodvorak
Andy Dorrell	www.culver.org/athletics-page
Andy Pedersen	www.southeasternswim.org
Angus Mugford	www.imgacademy.com
Ann Buck	www.twitter.com/AnnBuck10
Armstrong Family	
Anthony Boone	
Bill Parisi	www.parisischool.com
Bill Van Valer	www.stonycreekgolfclub.com
Boo Rigsbee	
Brandon Dhue	www.ontariobluejays.com
Brandon Gray	
Brett Hawke	www.auburntigers.com
Brian Griffits	www.spartaindy.com
Brian Hofman	www.onusports.com
Brian Satterfield	www.twitter.com/hseboysbball
Bryan & Jeff Smith	www.tennisprogram.com
Chad Odaffer	www.alteredphysique.com
Charles Rodgers	
Conrad Ray	www.gostanford.com
Corey Smallwood	www.goperformance.com
Correct2Compete Staff	www.correct2compete.com
Craig Haworth	www.winningyouthcoaching.com
Cris James	www.und.com
Dan Gould	www.educ.msu.edu
Daniel Jackson	
Darcy Rahjes	www.wlavikings.org
Dave Sickelsteel	www.rdsoffice.com
David Roux	www.davidrouxcoaching.com
Deeana Gumpf	www.und.com
Dennis Papadatos	www.gohofstra.com
Derrick Williams	www.menofthefamily.weebly.com
Doc O'Neal	www.prairieviewgc.com
Dr. Bernice Sorenson	www.onlychild.org.uk
Dr. Mark Robinson	www.amazon.com/Mark-Robinson
Dr. Robert A. Weil	www.sportsdoctorradio.com

Contributor	Website
Dr. Scotty Hamilton	www.elitesportspsychology.com
Duane Weber	www.thetrustpointe.com
Eddie Gill	www.allout-eddiegill.com
Emily Cohen	www.teamsnap.com
Frank Agin	www.frankagin.com
Floyd Keith	www.ppaservices.org
Greg Liberto	www.mymentalgamecoach.com
Hamilton Family	
Jake Gilbert	www.twitter.com/coachgilbert10
James Leath	www.jamesleath.com
Janis Meredith	www.jbmthinks.com
Jenn Bryden	www.fastpitchfit.com
Jenna Abraham	www.twitter.com/jennanicole33
Jennie Hebermehl Van Allen	
Jill Kramer	www.gofrogs.com
Jim Anthony	www.so-mark.com
Jim Thompson	www.positivecoach.org
Joe Jones	www.goterriers.com
Joe Skovron	www.twitter.com/skovy14
John Brubaker	www.coachbru.com
John Groce	www.fightingillini.com
John O'Sullivan	www.changingthegameproject.com
John Wingfield	www.ripfest.net
Jon Stutz	www.purgatorygolf.com
Justin Dehmer	www.1pitchwarrior.com
KC Woods	
Kelly Johnson	www.gopeacepacers.com
Kelsey Steuer	www.rugbyindiana.com
Kent Kinnear	www.usta.com
Kevin DeShazo	www.fieldhousemedia.net
Kevin Kennedy	
Kirk Mango	www.becomingatruechampion.com
Kristi O'Brien	www.brigadoonfitness.com
Kurt Schier	www.southerndunesgolfcourse.com
Kyle Lynn Veltri	www.und.com
Larry Lauer	www.usta.com
Levar Johnson	www.twitter.com/ljohnson26qbnwr
Marcus Amos	www.marcusamos.com
Mark James	
Marvin Cornish Jr.	www.linkedin.com/in/mbcornish1911
Maurice Hart	www.cortlandreddragons.com
Michael Mann	
Michelle Morton	
Mike Fleck	www.ballstatesports.com
Mike Christman	www.fitnessgarageindy.com
Mike Lingenfelter	www.munciana.com
Nicole Weller	www.nicoleweller.com

Don't Should on Your Kids

Contributor	Website
P.K. Gaeger	www.twitter.com/CoachGaegerRMU
Prairie View Academy	www.prairieviewgc.com
Quinn Barham	www.gopack.com
Renard Woodmore	
Rick & Julie Allen	www.informedathlete.com
Robert Taylor	www.smarterteamtraining.com
Rusty Kennedy	www.leavener.com
Ryan Sachire	www.und.com
Scott Haynes	
Scott Lien	
Scott McNealy	
Sean Bartram	www.corepilatesandfitness.com
Shaun Wines	
Shawn Jezek	www.linkedin.com/pub/shawn-jezek
Stephanie Hazlett	www.tennisprogram.com
Stu Singer	www.wellperformancecoach.com
Sue Poeschi	www.athletics.uwsp.edu
Susan Holt	www.und.com
Tim Roberts	www.thetrustpointe.com
Tariq Sbiet	www.northpolehoops.com
Tobais Palmer	
Tom Burchill	www.lawrenceswimteam.org
Tom Evangelista	www.sewaneetigers.com
Tommy Laurendine	www.sewaneetigers.com
Tony Monteleone	
Tony Pancake	www.crookedstick.org
Tyler Miller	www.forcebarbell.com
Tyler Russell	
Virgil Herring	www.virgilherring.com
Weslye Saunders	

Acknowledgments

Dr. Rob Bell:

First, thank you to Bill Parisi, who brought an incredible wealth of experience and perspective to this book. A special thank you to Will Drumright, an incredible person who goes above and beyond. He will become a cannon in the field of Sport Psychology. The interns—Hayden Reece, Bryanna Brugar, and Megan Melchiorre. Thank you to my amazing book designer, Teri Capron. Thank you to Derek Tow of South 40 media My family, Nicole, Ryan, and Porter, who live through it. I simply could not have done it without you. Love you! Thank you to God and Jesus Christ who made me redeemed, sanctified, and worthy.

Bill Parisi:

I would like to thank my partner on this project Dr. Rob Bell. His perseverance and tenacity to get this book done was the driving force to completing this manuscript. I have learned a great deal from him throughout this project.

To my wife Jennifer, and my two sons, William and Daniel. You have taught me, and continue to teach me, how to be a great sports parent. I have made my share of mistakes, like every parent, and I will probably make a few more. However every time I erred, you all were always there to accept and forgive. Life is about learning new strategies, and trial and error are a part of learning. My family is my rock and I love you more than anything in the world. Thank you for being a part of helping me deliver such important information.

To my parents, Mary and Nick. You have given me the most important thing any parent can give their child — unconditional love. You are always there for me and I aspire to be just like you with my own children.

To the entire Parisi Speed School network...all my fellow co-workers, strategic partners, facility owners, program directors, coaches, parents and most important, the athletes. If it were not for all of you, I would never be in the position to help Dr. Bell deliver these strategies. Your willingness to constantly improve motivates me everyday. I am blessed to be around and interact with so many great people.

Most important, I want to thank God. The Creator who has proven time and time again that with a strong faith, things always work out in the end...and realizing that if they don't, it's not the end.

Contents

Foreword

We all want the best for our children, but what does that mean when it comes to their sports and activities?

As an Olympic coach of the USA diving national training center for 15 years I have worked with many families and athletes from the talent identification process through Olympic games.

Our motto "from lessons to Olympians" puts us in a unique position of working with children from pre-adolescence through young adulthood. My experience has shown that the most well-rounded and best developed athletes come from families that are supportive and engaged but not vicarious in their approach to their child's sport.

With all of my background as an elite level coach for the United States, when it comes to your own child it is interesting how difficult it is sometimes to balance your wants for their success. I have often found myself reflecting and even biting my tongue on occasion as I parent my state champion daughter.

Dr. Rob Bell & Bill Parisi's approach towards this topic is positive, insightful, and inherently relative to our role as an athlete's parent. Don't Should On Your Kids brings to light many of the attributes that are necessary to assist your child in their athletic endeavors.

—JOHN V. WINGFIELD
2008 UNITED STATES OLYMPIC HEAD DIVING COACH

Introduction

Those who criticize this generation forget who raised it.

Somewhere, at some point, a change occurred in society. Some call it a perversion.

Youth athletics became professionalized. It became trophies over toughness, product over process, talent over tenacity, and winning over development. The death of backyard basketball and the slow fade of true open gyms gave way to structure, organization, and over-parented involvement.

The level of investment has increased and the expectations of the return of investment have followed suit. Maybe it is because no one has an ugly child or the emergence of elite under-ten travel teams. Perhaps it was the specialization of year-round athletes or tourney-cations instead of family vacations. Sprinkle in the absurd rising cost of tuition across universities and it makes sense—the talent and pressure have increased, and more is seemingly at stake. There is a systemic and malignant issue—the allure of the Division I scholarship.

- We have young athletes today who look like Greek gods in the batting cage, but can't effectively run the bases.

- There are more collegiate scholarships than ever offered to girls before they have driven a car.[1]

- We rank the number one 7th grade basketball player in the nation.

- Almost 45 million kids play at least one organized sport, but more than 85 percent quit before age fifteen.[2]

- Nearly half of all sport-related injuries at the high-school age are due to chronic overuse.[3]

- Parents will spend between $4,000 and $10,000 on athletics per year.[4,5]

- Young athletes will spend so much time invested in their sport that by the time they are sophomores in college, they won't understand why they are so tired all the time.

- Forty percent of male Division I basketball players will depart their initial school by the end of their sophomore year.[6]

At some point, the system created an attitude of What's in it for me? more than it did about the skills and life-lessons that sport can teach. We miniaturized long-term growth and development and maximized a short-term focus on winning or losing.

Unfortunately, a schism occurred in sports. Somewhere, the journey became more about the parents and the results than it did about the athletes and their growth. Like Jim Thompson, founder of the Positive Coaching Alliance stated, it created "perversion of potential."

Our kids became our trophies. We polished them off to show others and boasted proudly of their accomplishments. In doing so, kids became perfectionists and played safe. At some point, these athletes were not allowed to fail. They were judged too harshly on their mistakes—so much that they quickly discerned to just "not mess up." What fun!

This book is not intended to solve the issues around sports. It took a long time getting us into that mess and it would take a lot more to get us out. No, this book is to help build your child's mental toughness—a skill that will transfer into real life and go beyond their playing days.

Parents, we play a huge role in this area of development with our kids. As life becomes more complex and inundated with distractions, mental toughness becomes more important, yet also more complex. We may believe that back in the day was the 70's, 80's or even the 90's, but back in the day was ten years ago. Think about the vast differences our society has gone through since just ten years ago. How could we have adapted our parenting skills to the changes?

For most of us, our goal has been clear: We want our children to be happy, well adjusted and successful, for them to lead productive roles in society and make it a better place. When it is time for them to leave the nest—and leave they will (hopefully)—will they be ready? Our role is two-sided—we must enjoy each moment of them growing up and prepare them for eventual departure. That is our job.

Sadly, more parents are not allowing their kids to leave home. A new trend is when they leave for college; parents are following them to school, buying a place nearby. 6b This style of parenting unfortunately builds dependence, not independence. These actions display a lack of belief in their child's abilities to cope, deal, or handle adversity.

When our children were born, the clock grew legs. We turned around, and they were all grown up. That means we need to get serious about the business of shaping our kids and preparing them for their lives. Parents, we need to be their greatest supportive coach. It is our job to be the coach that we always wanted. Our actions shape their beliefs. We are the greatest influence on our children's lives and in their development, stability, attitudes, likes, and dislikes. Children watch everything we do and learn by modeling behaviors and beliefs about ourselves. Everything a parent does either reinforces a child's confidence or discredits their self-esteem. We shape their identities. Let's do it right.

This book will help.

Mental Toughness

Simple, but not easy.

One of the biggest misnomers is that sports are 90 percent mental. When we watch or play any sport, except for a few, it is something physical. Shooting a basket, throwing a pitch, sprinting, swimming, and so on, are physical. It's just that the remaining 10 percent is mental. It unhinges the other 90 percent, so if the 10 percent is not strong the other 90 percent is in vain.

Mental toughness is simple; it's just not easy. It's how we handle, cope, and deal with the setbacks and adversity. Mental toughness also involves how we perform under pressure; these "have to" moments. And it's only a matter of when, not if, these moments will occur.

We share with players and coaches that mental toughness will not win anyone a championship, but not having mental toughness will lose it. We are preparing for that one moment, and when our opportunity hits, it's too late to prepare.

Let's start with the end in mind. What is the goal of having our kids participate in sports? If the reason for playing is externally driven (such as a college scholarship,) then building mental toughness will be extremely difficult. Outcomes and external factors need to be the byproduct of sports, not the driver.

If the goal of playing is having fun and learning the skills needed in life, you're reading the right book. Having our youth and children become confident and resilient is the goal. We like to think that mental toughness is a result of sports, however it often just reveals it.

Mental toughness is not all or nothing. All or nothing is either/or thinking, black and white. All or nothing thinking means I'm either the best or I'm the worst. You're either first or you're last. We are the shark or the minnow, the Viking or the victim, the ulcer giver or the ulcer getter.

Addicts and perfectionists view life in all or nothing terms.

The difficulty with all or nothing thinking is that it is inherent in sports. We enjoy this part of athletics because it is unambiguous—there is a winner and a loser. Life isn't that way because there isn't a finish line, and there is much uncertainty. However, sport ONLY wants us to focus on the results. That's why "Did you win?" is the first question asked after any competition. We won or lost, got a hit or didn't, the best time or not, scored or didn't. All or nothing.

Mental toughness is getting away from all or nothing thinking and being able to focus on the process. It's about progress, not perfection.

Mental toughness is a continuum. It's not either I have it or I don't. Mental toughness is how much. How much mental toughness do I have left after making mistakes or after a bad performance? The skills that will translate into life are guts, resilience, and the willpower to fight and never give up.

Most people talk about mental toughness rather than instructing it. Coaches and programs that specifically address mental skills, character, and leadership are the ways that mental toughness is built.

Mental toughness, grit, or resilience is two-fold. The first part is how we handle, deal, and cope with adversity and setbacks. The second part is how well we perform under pressure. We are all going to face times of hardship, adversity, and struggle. These are inevitable. There will also be "have to" pressure moments. It is a matter of when, not if.

Mental toughness will be the deciding factor in one way or another for long-term success. Sure, some people may be inherently more mentally tough, just as some people are faster or better looking, but it still can be learned.

Don't "Should" On Your Kids

We take an adult view and impose it on our kids.

—Dr. Angus Mumford

An interesting thing occurs in every profession whether an ICU nurse, a grade school teacher, attorney or professor. When they are excellent at their job and possess talent, they are promoted. A nurse becomes an administrator, a grade school teacher becomes an assistant principal, an attorney makes partner, a professor becomes department head or dean, etc.

See, people get *should* on, even as adults. A nurse "*should* be an administrator." Maybe it is the right progression for them. However, a nurse's true passion may be working with patients, and becoming an administrator took her away from it. She realized later where her true passion resides, but she spent years doing what other people expected of her.

Our entire lives we have been *should* on. You should join the advanced program, you should double major, play the piano, play Division I, go into finance, become a president.

All of these positive "*shoulds*" are noble and well intentioned. It is great when people believe in you to have such high expectations. However, *shoulding* can get messy—and stink. It creates expectations to meet other's expectations. And these are just the positive types of *shoulds*.

As adults, we can hopefully recognize that, in most cases, people were just trying to provide advice and be helpful. However, when does *should* cross the line between helpful and hurtful?

Then there are the negative shoulds: You "*shouldn't*" wear that. You "*should*" call your mother more often. You "*shouldn't*" feel that way. You "*shouldn't*" make these mistakes. You "*should*" be more like your friend.

Does everyone know what's best for you? When others *should* on us, they are imposing their beliefs and experiences into our world. Making us feel like our experience, feelings, and beliefs don't matter that much. In reality, when people *should* on us, it's all about them and how they will somehow be affected by our actions or non-actions.

Parents who constantly *should* on their kids produce kids who *should* on themselves. If we were *should* on long enough and severe enough as a youth, the voice of should becomes internalized and we started *shoulding* on ourselves.

I "*should*" not have eaten that huge piece of cake last night. Maybe I *shouldn't* have said that. No, I definitely *shouldn't* have written that, etc.

When we conjure up feelings of "*should*," it doesn't motivate us. It does the opposite. A pile of *should* just reinforce the negative and reminds us that we are not good enough. See, I told you—you *shouldn't* have those negative thoughts!

Pain is temporary, but soreness lasts. We forget how full that one piece of cake made us feel. But, when reminded that we *shouldn't* have eaten it, it conjures up other feelings of how we *should* do better in other areas as well. The *shoulds* pile up. Directive statements about your child's past performances do little to inspire, instead creating fear. Condemnation, guilt, and shame are the result.

It's best to realize and be aware that a child will do almost anything to please his parents and his coach. When we *should* on our kids, we are establishing expectations, brutally reminding them of negatives, mistakes, and that they aren't good enough. When kids fail to reach your expectations, they can suffer and feel like a failure. *Shoulding* on them creates expectations that that they may or not be able to reach.

> *Alex, you **shouldn't** be nervous.*
>
> *Kristen, you have to play well today.*
>
> *John, you must perform better if you want to go further.*
>
> *Callie, you need to practice.*
>
> *Dwayne, you **shouldn't** make so many mistakes.*
>
> *Billy, whatever you do, don't make the last out.*

The title of this book reflects one of the strategies for building your child's mental toughness instead of tearing it down. The following pages will expand on and provide many more techniques. In this book, we don't demand that as a parent, you *should*, must, or have to execute these strategies. These recommended strategies are based on research and applied experience—it's up to you. However, you want to parent and coach, you've gotten this book for a reason, and athletics needs to remain about your son or daughter.

What do Wes Welker, Kurt Warner, Rod Smith, John Starkes, Warren Moon, London Fletcher, and Adam Vinatieri all have in common?

They will be hall of famers at some level, and all went undrafted. Why?

Speculation—it's the mother of all evil. Professional scouts are paid to evaluate talent and pick only the winners. It is such an inaccurate discipline that it has out of necessity become a combination of art and science. Scouts admit that they aren't always trying to hit home runs; they are interested in singles and doubles. However, scouts and organizations often still miss the mark on selecting the best. It's surface judgments based only on stats and performance, which are not a real predictor of success.

Likewise, trying to predict the eventual outcome of our son or daughter is futile. When immersed in the journey of sports development and success, try to start with the end in mind. But honestly, does the end you have in your mind mean a collegiate Division I scholarship? Beginning with the end in mind means visualizing the type of person we want our son or daughter to become.

The most important skill to learn from sport is mental toughness, grit, and resilience. The mental toughness of your son or daughter is largely due to how you parent, model your life, and surround them with a healthy environment. The arena of sport can provide the skills, ethic, ethos that we desire, and the life lessons that will transfer and permeate long after their career is over.

The foundations of this book are passion and confidence. However, drive, intrinsic motivation, perseverance, and persistence must come from your child. They must want it. They must be in touch with their own "why." It cannot come from us because it's hard to be driven when you're being driven.

Passion and confidence are the most important attributes in our children's development of mental toughness because it will become difficult at times. If they only play to please their parents or coach, for a scholarship or for pats on the back, it won't be enough. They will instead become "at-least," the subject of the next chapter.

Winners, Losers, and At-Leasters

The best coaching job is the head coach of an orphanage.

> *Wade was a very talented 12-year-old hockey player, but he was a coach's nightmare. He would only play hard when he felt like it, which was, unfortunately, only about a quarter of the time.*
>
> *Not surprisingly, Wade's father also worked whenever he felt like it. He had Dilbert comic strips up in his office and often bragged about how little he worked.*

Children will become in many ways what we as parents are, and we shape their belief systems. Most of us want our children to be better than ourselves and to have it better than we did. However, we cannot give away what we do not possess ourselves.

Let's oversimplify and say there are three types of people: winners, losers, and at-leasters. These are not only three types of people, but three distinct beliefs or mindsets that we form as children. They shape who we eventually become.

We love winners. For example, when anyone discusses athletes in life, no one talks about the 20th or 40th best athlete in that sport. They reference just a select few, the very best, the top 1/10 of 1 percent. Tiger Woods, Serena Williams, Tom Brady, Peyton Manning, LeBron James, and Missy Franklin, to name a few. They are referencing winners, athletic geniuses blessed to excel. These people will be successful in any situation.

Those perceived as losers, on the other hand, are born from a combination of poor circumstances and choices and a belief that everything turns out poorly for them. These are the victims of life. It never is about them; it's someone else's fault. Again, this represents a very small percentage of the population.

Most, however, are the at-leasters. At-leasters are not losers, far from it. They are involved, active, and in it. But, they lack the ingredients at becoming a winner. They believe that at-least we showed up, at-least we weren't last, at-least we weren't as bad as the other team. It's a defense mechanism that protects them from the pain of not being winners. It is a struggle for at-leasters to get out of their comfort zones. We have all been there, but we don't have to live there.

At-leasters go through the motions. Settling is okay. Playing it safe is good enough. Our comfort zone is too comfortable. We would rather be a maybe than a no. Be good, but not great. If we happened to be really good for one day, we dismiss it, saying, "Yeah, but I'm not *that* good."

The at-least mentality is toxic and systemic. The environment of youth sport has perpetuated at-leasters.

Youth sport that gives everyone a trophy has created an at-least mentality. At least we got a trophy… We don't create winners by making everyone **not** losers.

Youth sport often stresses winning so much over development that it has also created a culture of at-leasters. The short-term is magnified, and the long-term is miniaturized. The long-term is viewed through a telescope and the short-term through a microscope.

No one wants to lose, but when we only value winning over development, it causes us to self-protect. One way or another, "at least we weren't last" creeps into our mentality. We rarely create winners by only treasuring winning.

Athletes seek comfort and will do everything they can to please both coaches and parents. Athletes learn that the way to please coach and parents is to just not lose.

As a parent, we can inadvertently drive a child into the at-least mentality when we make it all about us. If this is one of your parenting techniques, remember—it's about them. We can't make it about us, and it cannot become about us. We fail when it becomes about us. The best sports parents seem to be behind the scenes, providing encouragement and a supportive environment. Appreciate the long-term, and depreciate the short-term.

No One Has an Ugly Child

It's tough to make predictions even about the future.

—*Yogi Berra*

No one has an ugly baby. It is tough to admit, but parents often lack the perspective and emotion to assess our own child's ability level accurately. We form an all or nothing mentality. We think they're either the best or that they are the worst.

It doesn't matter what you think of your child's ability level. We as parents over-estimate their ability and talent level. You're Mom and Dad—your role is to be supportive, not vicarious. Few scouts or recruiting directors will be calling you to ask how good you think your son or daughter is. Coaches will most likely observe the interactions among family members and how your son or daughter handles setbacks. What we value most, as a family, is on what we focus. Our role is to stress effort, accountability, character, and create a supportive environment—not measure their vertical leap, bat speed, or split times.

> Mrs. Riggs was a walking scorer at a PGA event, one of those who keep track of each shot a player hits. After the round, she made it a point to call this PGA player's father and tell him what a mature, class act his son was. She didn't have to call, but what greater compliment could a father receive than unsolicited praise about his son's character. And this was from one afternoon of interactions during a round of professional golf.

Do not hesitate to share with others the positives about someone else. By the same token, resist the urge to tell others how talented your child is. Allow others close to your child to boast about him or her. Hopefully, they describe an aspect of your child's character, rather than just their talent. We often forget that youth sports are intended to build character and serve as a metaphor for life.

Vicarious vs. Supportive

Do you live through your child or with your child?

Your child is having a great season as the post-season approaches. He is worried. He asks you the question, "What if I lose?"

What is your response?

A *vicarious parent* would reply along the lines of, "That's not going to happen, you're so good" or "You shouldn't think that way." If you're a parent who responds this way, you're likely living directly through your child's success or failure. You still mean well and love your kid, but you've just become too emotionally invested in the results.

These types of parents, unfortunately, lack the perspective to make rational decisions. They live and die with every play and game. Their child is the best when he or she wins, and they are the worst when they lose. All or nothing.

- Vicarious parents are as close as physically possible to every practice.

- Vicarious parents often blame others when the important outcomes do not go well.

- Vicarious parents are the ones comparing their son or daughter to others.

- Vicarious parents stress out quickly and easily.

- Vicarious parents are usually the ones at the games shouting instructions.

- Vicarious parents feel their child's success is a reflection of themselves.

- Vicarious parents don't realize they are living through their child.

A *supportive parent*, on the other hand, answers the "What if I lose?" question a different way. They approach along the lines of, "Why do you think that?" or "Let's talk it through…what if you lose?" Supportive parents provide an environment that remains safe. They don't try to solve their kids concerns. They encourage their children to think for themselves, come up with their solutions and handle their outcomes. Home is not a fan base. Athletes can rest assured that in the home, no matter how they perform, their identity is not just as an athlete. They have unconditional love and support. Lastly, these children aren't nagged about their preparation or whether they are nervous before important performances.

- Supportive parents attend from a distance and may even miss a practice.

- Supportive parents ensure their son or daughter assumes responsibility, not blaming coaches or situations.

- Supportive parents stress effort over results.

- Supportive parents know their son or daughter's performance is just a shadow of them, not a reflection.

- Supportive parents make sure they aren't over the top.

- Supportive parents are aware of the long-term development.

- Supportive parents don't *should* on their kids.

Both types of parents make sacrifices and difficult decisions for their child along the journey. No one questions whether the love and support are there. Unfortunately, these vicarious or supportive labels are not mutually exclusive. We may sometimes be one type of parent with one child and another type with another. It's possible for the pendulum to swing to both extremes and even for us to live in the middle. This is about progress, not perfection. We are going to make mistakes, but that is the point. How can we help our child build mental toughness? How can we become better, more self-aware parents in the process?

When you think about parents of famous athletes, who comes to mind? Was it a parent that stayed behind the scenes or one that sparked controversy?

Archie and Olivia Manning are examples of successful sports parents. The couple produced two number-one overall NFL draft picks, two Super Bowl winning quarterbacks, and two Super Bowl MVPs. Archie Manning said it best, *"We just tried to raise good kids and have a good family. I don't like the perception that it (having the boys play pro football) was a plan."*[7]

On the opposite end of the spectrum, a mother of a collegiate basketball player uttered these words to the head coach when asked about her son's goals, *"My goals are his goals."* Okay, then.

Three Types of Parents

Most parents build dependency, great parents build capacity.

All parents want the absolute best for their child. The easy tell of a parent's confidence is to watch them during their child's competition. The most confident parents are relaxed and not stressing at all. Those who lack self-confidence are uptight, pacing, and even providing instructions.

Parents who are comfortable in who they are, their identity, and their roles in life produce children who are comfortable, confident, and relaxed. However, parents who are truly insecure reflect that insecurity at home to their kids. They should on their kid, because they need them to be successful to make somehow up for their feelings of insecurity.

The Simple Parent

The first type of parent knows very little about their kid's sport. And these are often the best types of parents. They were never gymnasts or tennis players, so they are unable to provide any knowledgeable feedback.

Of course, there are also those who never played, so they think it is different and easier than it is. It is funny and sad to watch a parent who knows jack donuts about the sport they are trying to teach when they can't even do it themselves.

The Assistant Coach

The second type of parent is the one who played sports. They achieved some success, but may not have achieved what they thought to be their full potential. They are knowledgeable on how they approached and played the game. Since they know the answers, these are often the most vicarious type of parent because they are smart enough to be very dangerous. These parents criticize more than they commend and point out the one mistake rather than the many positives.

The Success

A third type of parent is the former elite athlete. They can be very hands-off, knowing full well the sacrifices that need to be made for success. If the typical parent knew what it took to be a professional athlete, they wouldn't sign up—for their kids or themselves. These former athletes are aware that it must be about their child and helping them develop their own passion. They do allow their son or daughter to experience failure because they know how instructive it can be. However, they can also place high expectations on their child because of their own past successes.

If you recognize yourself in the above descriptions, take some advice: Allow coaches to do the tough coaching. That's not your role. Coaches are the ones who can and should provide the appropriate feedback. Too often, athletes receive one message from the coach on a technique or strategy, only to have parents provide their interpretation and feedback that contradicts the coach. This is confusing for the child, who may feel torn over what to do.

Three Types of Athletes

Show me an athlete afraid to look bad, and I'll show you an athlete you can beat every time.

—Unknown

The Safe Perfectionist

The first type of athlete is the safe perfectionist. This type of athlete has become the new normal. Playing it safe is the way to maintain the appearance of perfectionism. However, perfectionism is another word for insanity.

> The point guard at this university was a good player, made few mistakes, and played consistently. However, he often held back and never took over a game. As a result, the team bowed out early during the postseason. This player never reached his potential.

Athletic directors and coaches stress one huge change in recent years. More and more athletes have become perfectionists, safe, and afraid to make mistakes. They struggle with handling adversity and being able to make adjustments.

From helmets used in soccer, face-masks for fielding, and mouth guards galore, we have become overly concerned about an athletes safety. In some cases, this is justified. However, when it comes to reaching our potential, safe doesn't cut it. Playing it safe is risky. The safe perfectionist plays not to lose, rather than to win.

The safe perfectionist is afraid of messing up. She knows she can play it safe and not get judged too harshly nor risk defeat through her play. Playing it safe means she will not be called out, and she can't be the one who is blamed if a loss occurs. The motivation to put yourself *out there* simply does not outweigh the risk of defeat.

At some point, these athletes became afraid to fail! They were judged too harshly on their mistakes or put way too much pressure on themselves. The athlete quickly discerned to do their best not to mess up.

Vicarious parents often unconsciously contribute to the safe perfectionist athlete, as we only pointing out the negative or comparing their performance to someone else. Vicarious parents struggle with praise and feel pushing their child is the only way to long-term success.

Building mental toughness in your child means helping them to play their best when it matters the most. There is a saying that "if it bleeds, it leads." Sport is the arena where our kids should learn how to put themselves out there, go for it, lead from the front, and play with whatever passion is in their hearts. Nervousness, excitement, and risk exist when you're putting everything on the line. As Billy Jean King stated, "pressure is a privilege."

Mental toughness is also how we all learn to deal and cope with adversity. These are the skills to emphasize in youth sports. Mental toughness is paramount beyond the field of play, assuming the goal is to build skills that transfer into life. When we face pressure moments, will we play it safe or have the confidence to take the risk?

> The first female billionaire and inventor of Spanx, Sara Blakely, reported her secret to success was the influence of her father. She was encouraged by failing, because failing means you are trying, and she learned from her dad that true failure meant not trying at all. She credits what she learned from her father to her success because she wasn't intimidated later in life, taking a risk in the massive field of retail—and pushing through to become a success.[8]

Game Day or Practice Day Athlete

Watch this or don't miss?

Two other types of athletes are the game day athlete and the practice day athlete.

Game day athletes are the ones who don't particularly practice that hard, but they show up on game day. What frustrates coaches is their true potential is never realized. These are the athletes with talent. The issue is that we have no idea that athlete is going to show up on game day—it could be Taylor Swift or Lady Gaga, Tom Cruise or Adam Sandler. There is little consistency in their performance. Game day athletes can be great at times, but they *could* be the very best. Depending on their ability level the next level is often a huge awakener for them because everyone is good, yet they may lack the dedication that it takes to get there and stay there.

Practice day athletes, on the other hand, are the ones who practice the best and usually work the hardest. They are ones who complete every pass in practice, shoot the lowest scores before the tournament, and have killer pick-up games.

But when the lights turn on, for some reason, their confidence fizzles. Practice day athletes shrink and morph into the type of player who goes from "watch this" to "I hope I don't miss."

From a parent's perspective, these types will wear you out and can be frustrating. You've seen their best and you're aware of their potential, but they don't always play that way.

Vicarious parents do much harm with either of these athletes. They want consistent and progressive results and stress out and blame others when playing levels off. The *shoulds* often occur during these times.

Supportive parents do their best parenting with these types. They can notice when their son or daughter is not doing as well as hoped. They want to help, and remain objective and empathize rather than judge or question their effort level. Supportive parents point out success, no matter how small.

The path may be troublesome and setbacks will occur, many of which are inevitable. It is a curvy path toward mastery, not a straight line. Allow the coaches to do their craft, and remain supportive. This isn't a snap your fingers kind of revelation, but a process that evolves sometimes quickly, sometimes slowly.

Confidence—Prepare Them for the Hinge Moment

Every door has a hinge; if it doesn't, it's just a wall.

The pilot of an AirBus A320 took off from La Guardia airport on a flight to Charlotte. Less than three minutes into the flight, the plane with 155 passengers aboard struck a flock of geese and immediately lost both engines and all power to the airplane. The pilot immediately knew that he couldn't get back to the airport and needed to find a place to land the plane in the most populated area in the entire world. The incident became known as the miracle on the Hudson, as Captain Chelsey "Sully" Sullenberger successfully landed the plane on the Hudson River.

Throughout Captain Sully's more than forty years of flying and 20,000 hours of airtime, he had achieved his goal of never crashing an airplane. What he didn't and couldn't realize is that his entire life had been in preparation for that one moment. Who else would you have wanted piloting that airplane?[9]

The Hinge: The Importance of Mental Toughness was written because in every one's life there are significant moments. In every important game, the outcome is usually decided by one play. At the highest level, an entire season is dictated by one game. The hinge is that one play, game, event or person that makes all the difference in our lives. We do not know when it will happen or who it will be, except in retrospect.

The importance of mental toughness is that it only takes one. It doesn't matter how poorly we played last season, how we messed up last game or even the last play. It only takes one play or game to turn everything around! We need to be mentally tough because when our opportunity hits, it's too late to prepare. We need to be ready.

The hinge connects who we are with who we become. Although it only takes one, there will be many possible hinge moments in our lives.

An interesting aspect of hinge moments is that we are not aware of them until after they occur, which may be days, weeks, months, or even years after they occur. We can't connect the dots looking ahead; we can only connect them looking backward.

Unfortunately, a lack of mental toughness can keep the hinge from connecting. If we lack the ability to refocus, play with confidence, or handle adversity, then we will likely miss the most important play, the next one. We prepare for the few moments that decide the outcome of the game.

We can't predict the future, we can only prepare for the unpredictable. Since we have no idea which moments or games or people will make all the difference, we need to treat every game and moment as a possible hinge moment.

Parenting Hinge Moments

It only takes one.

John Starks played only one year of high school basketball and went undrafted out of college. He played in the independent leagues of basketball and even played a season in the NBA for the Golden State Warriors. However, no one could have predicted that he would become a NBA all-star and the New York Knicks all-time leader in three-pointers. It was an injury that led him to Knicks stardom.

He received a try-out with the Knicks but wasn't expected to make the team. Fortune favors the bold and Starks had plenty of that intangible skill. During try-outs, his 6'3" frame attempted a dunk over 7'0" Patrick Ewing. The hall of fame center rejected the dunk and slammed Starks to the ground, causing Starks to injure his knee. NBA rules state that a player cannot be cut from a roster if they are injured, so he remained on the team. It was after he returned that the Knicks began to value his work ethic so much that he garnered playing time. His injury became a hinge moment.[10]

It doesn't matter where your children are on the depth chart, or how bad things seem. We need to stay ready because it only takes one! For our hinge to connect, we must have confidence.

People think that most hinge moments are only in big games. It's true, games hold important moments; however many occur in practice, in normal games or even on the ride home. Once an athlete makes the connection with their true confidence or they figure something out, these serve as hinge moments. These are the events that transcend the world of sports and into everyday life skills.

Can the ride home be a hinge moment? Remember the old rhyme, *"Sticks and stones may break my bones, but words will never hurt me?"* That lie ranks right alongside with, *"Don't worry, that ball won't hurt."*

What hurts worse than someone criticizing us, especially someone close to us? Words can cause emotional scarring. We have to be careful about what we say to our loved ones because they are listening. If we continually criticize and mention only the negatives from a performance and how they need to get better, then that is what they will hear and focus on.

A golf instructor mentioned how a father of a player told him that he was playing great, but "pulled a Sara, I choked on the last hole." Sara, his daughter, directly heard it, and the instructor said that you could see the confidence leak out of her. How many times had she heard that label, and what kind of self-concept did she have?

We cannot build up certain moments or games because this only makes athletes tight and try to force things to happen. We need to stress that effort is everything. Our effort in practice and in games where we are behind or the season is going poorly. These are hinge moments as well. Unfortunately, tragedies are immediate and powerful hinges. From that moment on, everything is changed. It doesn't mean that it has to remain bad, but things have changed.

The death of a loved one, cancer, accidents, and natural disasters are examples of tragedies. Making an error, missing a shot, or messing up are not any fun at all and will hurt, but they are still just challenging experiences in comparison.

There is an important difference between tragedies and challenging experiences. This may be difficult, but no matter how bad an outcome is in sports, even at the highest level, it is a challenging experience—it is not a tragedy. Failure is never fatal. It may feel like it for a while, but it is only a challenge. Keeping athletics in the proper perspective for our children helps them keep their problems in perspective.

And as your son or daughter reflects back and connects the dots on these challenging experiences, it will be their mental toughness that defines their success. Sometimes the biggest setbacks in life can be setups for the biggest comebacks. Overcoming challenging experiences is what helps our children grow.

Ann was a dancer who started at a young age and had goals of becoming the prima ballerina for a ballet company. As a young girl, her coach also had a daughter who danced and competed. Sadly, this coach favored her own daughter a bit more over Ann and began to slowly chip away at Ann's self-confidence throughout the years. Anyone who has been on the opposite end of being a coach's favorite understands what this feels like.

Ann's parents were of course empathetic. It pained them to watch their daughter struggle with her chosen passion. They listened and supported her but they also built Ann's mental toughness. Ann's parents refused to directly intervene. They allowed Ann to work out the issues on her own. Her parents had a rule that once Ann chose to commit to a season she could not quit. They remained supportive, but not vicarious.

It was extremely painful experience for Ann at the time, but the lessons would prove to be fruitful. Her mental toughness garnered from overcoming challenges in her sport had effectively prepared for her professional career.

Confidence is King, Focus is Queen

This is chess—this isn't checkers.

In the movie *Training Day*, Denzel Washington has a great line where he says, "This is chess—this isn't checkers." Sport and life are the same way. There are no grand masters in checkers. However, I'm sure there are a lot of ties. We quit playing checkers because it's no longer a challenge. In chess, however, there are a lot of moving parts and no ceiling.

Confidence is king because the lack of confidence is how games are lost. When the king dies the game is over. Once we lose confidence or trust in coaches, our parents or ourselves it is difficult to get it back. If confidence is lost at the elite levels of the sport, the game is over.

The king in chess does not win the game. The king only moves one space at a time. Likewise, confidence is a fragile commodity. It can take weeks and months to build it up, but only one poor choice of words on our part as a parent to tear it down.

Focus is queen. The game is won by moving our queen. We gain confidence by addressing our focus. Whatever we focus on grows. When we play and practice, where and what do we focus on?

If athletes focus on messing up, try **not** to make a mistake or playing it safe, then their lack of confidence will grow. If they label themselves as a slow starter, poor finisher or an at-leaster, then this focus becomes their reality. On the other hand, if athletes are focused on the next play in front of them, making a play, and staying aggressive, confidence grows and success is the result.

Confidence is a Feeling

*Pressure can burst a pipe, but we think
it only produces diamonds.*

If you ask any athlete what they're thinking about when they're playing at their best, the answer is always the same: "Nothing." Athletes that achieve mind-blowing streaks in any sport when asked how they did it also say: "I don't know."

Elite performers all stress that when they are playing their best, the event slows down. They feel in complete control. Have you ever finished a workout or a run, looked at yourself in the mirror and thought, "Hey, I look good." Honestly, you look no different from when you began, except you now feel different. Depending on our perspective on spirituality, our prayers may not be automatically answered, but we feel better after praying or even meditating. We feel at peace.

When an athlete loses confidence that feeling now turns into thoughts. They just begin to think too much. They no longer trust their instincts, their gut. Instead, they get stuck inside their head and try to think their way into right acting. The first thing that goes when an athlete begins performing poorly is the lack of feeling. Their play or technique may look fine, but if they don't feel confident, they will begin to search.

Confidence eventually becomes the most important part of mental toughness because it affects all other skills. Our children will attempt and continue to participate in activities where they feel successful. Confidence extends to include our children's belief and trust in those around them, coaches, and parents.

Confidence is not only a feeling, however. Mental toughness means being able to play well when our feeling is off. There will be days and weeks that are tough, and due to many different circumstances, the athlete doesn't feel confident. They lose that trust and belief. Hopefully at that time, your child's confidence is plugged into something greater than their performance.

Research has shown that there are various sources of confidence. Sport psychology coaches teach ways to become confident by changing our physiology, our body language, and how we feel. If confidence wasn't a feeling, then why stress focused breathing or becoming centered?

Build Confidence Through Their GPS

We do not know the results from our action,
but if we take no action, there will be no results.

—*Gandhi*

How many of us have been driving in an unfamiliar place, following our GPS, and we suddenly felt that we were not quite in the right spot? So, we turned a corner or drove straight ahead disregarding the map.

Our confidence is our built-in GPS system. Trust is our gut, our intuition, and the belief and ability to trust in our decisions. Confidence is the ability to re-focus, to let go of mistakes, and to listen to our gut, our inborn GPS. Our GPS points us in the direction we are supposed to go. It's our decision whether or not to trust our gut.

Here's what our GPS does not do, however. I've never had the GPS ask me, How did you get here? Why are you in this part of town? Are you going to be late? Our GPS merely redirects us if we miss a turn or take a different route.

Confidence doesn't judge. It never asks questions like, How did you get in this situation? This should be over, why are you even here? Are you really good enough?

Parent Strategy: Program their GPS

Has your child ever asked, "don't you trust me?" One of the myths of trust is like mental toughness; it's not all or nothing. The myth is that we have it, or we don't. Trust is a continuum. Does it become a question of *how much do I trust*? For example, we may trust our kids to drive the car, but not across the country.

Trust is a process… How much do we trust our kids? Trust affects everything because the more we trust and have confidence, the better focused, relaxed, and honest we become. If we give someone a task and know that it will be done, it frees us up to focus on something else.

One of the best traits that we can share with our kids is trust. How much do we trust our gut and our instincts?

Build your son or daughter's GPS by allowing them the choice to listen to it or not. Allow them to make mistakes and learn from it to problem solve and find a way. It's not easy. However, we fail to be a GPS ourselves when we start judging their performance, overly questioning their effort or always fixing it for them.

We confuse our inborn GPS when we become unable to let go of mistakes and bring up past errors. It is difficult, if not impossible, to remain confident if we can't redirect ourselves on the destination and how to get there.

We need to build up and learn to trust our inborn GPS so we can be the steady guide for our children. Listening to our gut is a skill and requires that we remain in the moment and take action.

> There was a parent who no matter what her daughter suggested would offer up the worst possible outcome. The girl was in college and had been hearing this negativity her entire life! It's not a shock that she became unable to trust any decision she made on or off the field. She was very talented but had low detrimental confidence. When things would go wrong in sport, she could not make adjustments.

Bad outcomes, bad breaks, and inconveniences will happen. These are inevitable. The way we build mental toughness in our kids is by allowing them to go through these tough periods and find a way.

However, if we do not take any action there will be no results. If we don't first trust our GPS then we can't give it away.

Confident people can do this skill.

Don't Should on Your Kids

Nothing Bothers You

Body language doesn't talk, it screams.

October 14th, 2003, Game six of the National League Championship Series between the Chicago Cubs and the Florida Marlins. This was supposed to be the year that ended the 95-year World Series drought for the Cubs. There was uneasiness in the crowd even though Mark Prior was pitching great that day, having allowed only three hits going into the eighth inning. The Cubs were leading 3-0 in the game and one win away from taking the series. In many ways, Cubs fans were waiting for it to take a turn for the worse.

What happened in the eighth inning became known as "the Steve Bartman incident." Moises Alou had a chance to catch Louis Castillo's foul ball, in which Cubs fan Bartman tried to catch it as well, denying Alou and the Cubs the second out of the inning. All the fans in the stadium and even the players didn't pay much attention to the actual play, until seconds later, when Moises Alou had a mini-tantrum, lost his cool, slammed his glove, and yelled at the fan. The reaction by Alou communicated to everyone, PANIC. Only then did the entire crowd know and the air completely left the stadium.

It was his reaction to the event that led to a horrible response.

Mark Prior next threw a wild pitch and then shortstop Alex Gonzalez made an error to load the bases. At the end of the inning, it was 8-3 in favor of the Marlins, who won the series the following game.[11]

Body language doesn't talk, it screams. Sometimes it swears.

Now what-if never happened, but had Alou not reacted, the team might have kept their cool and the Marlins may not have been so inspired and relentless.

Think about how real confidence looks and acts? Chances are we mostly think of someone playing well and dominating the sport. Confidence comes naturally at these moments.

The truth is that everyone faces adversity, struggles, and goes through dry spells. This can come in the form of struggle during a game or adversity throughout a season. Can we have confidence during these times as well?

Confidence is the most important part of mental toughness and a true indicator of how an athlete handles the struggle. It's how we handle the struggle and how our children interact with us during these times of stress.

Confidence is simply the belief that it will work out. Fear is the biggest barrier to confidence because we don't believe that it is going to work out like we want it. Playing time, scholarships or failing can all put stress on the confidence level of our children.

The best let nothing bother them. They keep their head in the game when others are losing theirs. They believe in their process so much that they refuse to let setbacks affect their mindset or their team. It's amazing to see, but the best athletes manage their poise and focus. Nothing bothers them. It is the major impact of confidence and the true test of one's level of confidence and mental toughness.

It is common for the major changes or setbacks to bother us. However, ever notice when we get stressed that everything seems to bother us like the person next to us in traffic or our family? When we are confident, these things don't bother us at all but they become the first thing to annoy us when we lose our belief that things will work out.

When we criticize others outside of our family our children hear this. When we become stressed out and we struggle to control our language or behavior, our children witness it. As coach John Brubaker states, "Parenting is contagious." We can't give away what we don't have and if we get uncomfortable our kids will follow suit.

During games most of the poor behavior by parents is because they feel everything must go their way—meaning no bad calls, all the playing time, no drama on the team, and certainly no mistakes. If the goal is to have nothing bad happen during the game, then have your son or daughter play for the Globetrotters, because they're the only team that never loses.

When we lose our cool during a game or criticize after the game, we show our children that we don't believe things will work out. If we did, then we wouldn't let it bother us so much. We still may get upset, but we can refocus, not let it bother us, and certainly not reflect this behavior to our kids.

We can make this mantra a goal to be achieved rather than just an outcome of confidence. The only way we can achieve our goal of *nothing bothers me* is if we are confident. What we agree to is the belief that "I don't need everything to go my way to be successful. I believe it will work out, and I am just going to act as if."

Pre-Season

Pre-season is a time to help build a child's mental toughness. Parents should be saluted during this time of the year because it is not easy. We often contribute the most amount of sacrifice during these times. You have contributed to the cause financially, through car rides, and through multiple conversations about how to make everything work.

The theme of mental toughness during this time of the year is MOTIVATION.

The goal is for them to want it more than you. How do you achieve that? Our job is to allow them to take ownership in their development. Encourage their efforts and compliment them on improving. Most importantly, keep the pre-season in perspective. Don't focus on rankings, predictions or the "what if's" of a season. Instead, focus on the process and having fun. But beware, because the *shoulds* often start to emerge during this time of the season. You *should* have a great season. You *should* work on your weaknesses. Or, this is an important year; you *should* have a good one. These statements put emphasis on the wrong goal. Keep it about the process and keep it positive.

It's Not Who Can Get There First — It's Who Can Get There And Stay There

Have you ever drank wine before it's ready?

—Mike Lingenfelter

Let's compare the journeys of two youth athletes. Remember the player as a youth who somehow had a beard? Typically the best athletes at younger ages are the biggest and the most physically developed. But golf is a sport where physical development is less important and occurs much later. It's such a mental game, so this kid had a proverbial mental beard. He played beyond his years, didn't make mistakes, and won—a lot.

He was not only the number-one 12-year-old golfer in California, but he was so good that at one international tournament he shot 73-70 and won it by 16 shots. When he finished 6th at the Junior World Golf Championships that same year, the best field in the world, he was disappointed. At that time in California future PGA champion Rickie Fowler looked up to this kid.

As a freshman in high school, every collegiate program wanted this golfer and everyone approached him. The expectations for this young man were tremendous and he admitted that when he began to struggle he thought he was letting everyone down. When growth occurred his golf swing changed, he became confused with mechanics, started enjoying other sports, and soon lost confidence. Remember, confidence is king.

Luckily, his stellar grades buffered him from finding his complete identity in being only a golfer. He still managed to play in college but at a much lower level. This golfer's name, Joe Skovron, would actually later become Rickie Fowler's caddy on the PGA Tour.

In comparison, the other youth athlete played all different competitive sports at a younger age, including football, baseball, and basketball. Everyone in the state of Indiana played basketball and his dad played basketball in college struggling somewhat when he stopped playing.

The expectation was never for this kid to play professional golf. He didn't start playing competitive golf until 12 years old, much later than other professional golfers. The expectations from every round of golf were to have fun, learn something, have a positive experience, and make a friend. In an 8th grade tournament, he shot an 89 in the first round. In the car ride, they didn't discuss the round at all—only the excellent par on the last hole. He responded by shooting a 71 the next day.

Patrick Rodgers' development and passion for golf took off in high school. His dad and mom always allowed golf to be their son's passion. Patrick ended up playing golf at Stanford, tied Tiger Woods' record with eleven wins, became the number-one ranked collegiate golfer, won the Ben Hogan award, and turned professional after his junior season.

> The Super Bowl features the best two teams and many of the best players in the NFL. Super Bowl XLIX between the New England Patriots and the Seattle Seahawks was epic. An interesting fact about that Super Bowl was that not one starter on either team was a five-star recruit.[12]
> As golf professional Virgil Herring said, "It's not who gets there first; it's who can get there and stay there."

For smaller schools participating in basketball, making the NCAA tournament is a successful season even though the sport provides the most upsets in major collegiate sports. In 1999, Weber State University in Utah won the Big Sky Conference and was awarded a 14-seed and a 3rd seed opponent powerhouse, University of North Carolina (UNC). North Carolina was making its 25th consecutive tournament and hadn't lost a first round game since 1978.

A star was introduced to the country that day. Harold Arceneaux led Weber State with 36 points and with two free throws in the closing seconds, beat 3rd seeded UNC. It remains as one of the biggest upsets in tournament history, and the last time Weber State won an NCAA tournament game.

Although Weber State lost their next game to the University of Florida in overtime, Harold Arceneaux scored 32 points. He declared for the NBA draft, but instead returned to Weber State for his senior season, against the recommendations of many NBA scouts.

Due to Harold Arceneux returning for his senior season, NBA scouts were at most games, and they began to notice his teammate, Eddie Gill. Eddie was also a senior and by all accounts, was the 2nd best player on the Weber State team. Arceneaux was awarded Big Sky player of the year, whereas Gill was 1st team all-Big Sky Conference.

Both players were heavily scouted and received invitations to the many select pre-NBA draft camps. However, due to the bizarre nature of scouting neither player was drafted. Arceneaux never played one NBA game but Gill went on to have an 8-year NBA career. The difference wasn't talent, it was something else. It's not who gets there first; it's who can get there and stay there.

We are only as good as our practice and our passion toward it. The passion of a player translates into their dedication, work ethic, and overall mentality. These are the intangibles of a player that cannot be measured effectively. The story of Gill is one of persistence that is often manifested throughout all sports at all levels.

Can't Want It More Than Them

It all works out in the end. If it hasn't, it's just not the end.

Dale Earnhardt, the hall of fame race car driver was once in a terrible accident. It was so bad that he could not finish his next race at Indianapolis Motor Speedway. He started the race but they had to remove him from the car. Here was the greatest race car driver, basically crying because they had to take him out of the car. He said, *"Nobody loves anything more than my driving a race car."*

The best love to play.

They possess an unquenchable thirst to see how good they can become, and they enjoy the process of it. I'm not certain when exactly this passion, tenacity, and drive are born. I think mental toughness is something that's caught more than it's taught.

Herschel Walker was made fun of at school and never went out to recess because he was afraid of getting beat up. His teacher used to put him in the corner of the room because he had a speech impediment and called him "special." His father used to give him a quarter to buy a snack at school. Herschel would instead give it to another kid, so they could buy a snack as long as they would talk to him. After the kid had finished his snack, he would go back to making fun of him.

The last day of school in 8th grade, he went out to recess and got beat up, bad. He said to himself, *"never again. When your name is called, you have to stand up."*

From that hinge moment in school, he didn't train to become a great athlete, he trained to become a superhero. How did he do it?

Herschel did about 5,000 sit-ups and 5,000 push-ups every day. He also ran on a dirt track every day with a rope tied around his waist dragging a tire. He transformed himself from one of the slowest guys in the school to one of the fastest in the state of Georgia by the 9th grade.[13]

Consider this example: Imagine if a parent told their child they had to do Herschel's workout.

Most champion athletes did not start out in the sport with the aspirations of being an elite champion athlete. They played a variety of sports and only after they fell in love with the sport and showed potential did they develop champion athlete aspirations.

As parents, there is a fine line between wanting to show our kids the path and wanting to clear the path. Mental toughness means helping equip them to encounter the struggles, adapt, and persevere. Their path can only be accomplished in pursuits that we love.

The idea of arranged marriages in the United States is unthinkable. But, we now seem to approach sports this way. We bought into the idea that kids need to pick a sport and stay with it.

Dating is a risk, but matrimony is a bigger risk. We love romance because it involves dating, courtship, talking, and sharing. However, is the first person you fall in love with the same person you're with today? Allowing younger children to experiment and sample a variety of sports is healthy and encourages them to choose eventually the one they love.

The systems in place may try to steer you toward year-round sport, which involves little off-season and no time for any other sport. The lines may even come across as "if they want to play at the next level, then…" The organizations in place are also tiered for longer and longer seasons. If they do well at a tournament, they are invited to another and so on. Tournaments are a multi-billion dollar industry so it's in their best interests for your son or daughter to pick their sport.

Specializing any time before the age of 12 is a gamble. Yes, it occurs, and a few of these athletes are successful; however, this is a major outlier. We honestly don't know the precise age where specialization should or should not occur. Different governing bodies set various standards. Of course there are exceptions, but the point is to allow them to discover their true passion.

We receive calls every week from parents wanting our mental coaching for their son or daughter. We discuss the goals and struggles. We also discuss ways parents can get better as a sports parent (hence, this book). Near the end of these introductory calls is the screening of each parent, with one question, "*Is this something your child wants?*"

If the child initiates the possibility of mental training, then we have a good chance of success. If the parent hasn't even asked their son or daughter about mental training—forget about it. It won't work.

Whatever the situation, they have to want it—period. No matter the sport, the best athletes have to possess **passion**. They don't have to be asked to work at it, nagged to do something or coerced into it. And that's the way it should be. Wait, did we just *should* on you?

What's Your Why?

Our why must make us cry. If it doesn't, it's not our why.

The first question we ask athletes working on their mental game is, "Why do you play?" It is a powerful question and we receive a variety of answers. They commonly answer with *the competition*, *the fun*, and *the camaraderie* or *the friendships*. Delving deep into someone's "why" for playing, one thing gets revealed: The reason they began playing is often not the same reason they are playing now.

The why uncovers someone's real desire for playing and can unlock some of the small performance issues. I have only come across one kiss of death for someone's why and that is, "I'm good at it." Being good at something can increase the enjoyment for certain, but it's not a powerful enough reason because at some point everyone is good. Eventually their why catches up with them.

They play because they are good at it, and they win. Along with the winning brings the pats on the back, the cheers, and an athletic identity of "This is who I am." It's not a powerful enough why, at some point they are no longer the best, they don't win all the time, and many times they didn't work on their weaknesses while they were dominating. If they don't have a deeper reason for playing and it is no longer fun, they can become stagnant in their development. The worst is the collegiate athlete who is good, but no longer enjoys their sport and now feels trapped.

Parent Strategy: Know Your Own Why

Whatever you value the most in life is how you'll parent. You will make decisions based on these values. For instance, if your values in life are family and money, then the balance between career and travel will be a factor in your decision. Whatever you decide will reveal which priority is number one. It's not realistic to have both.

Why do you want your child involved in the sport? What do you value most from having your kids play youth sports? If it is the benefits that sport, coaching, and the lessons it can provide, then tough decisions will follow your values. If you value achievement, opportunities for your child, and playing at the *next level*, then most decisions will be based on these values. It's difficult to have both of these as the motivation because we either focus on the process or the product. One of these "why's" becomes the driver, while the other "why" sits in the backseat.

Scholarship as the Byproduct

Wake up [parents], we've got the dreamer's disease.

—*New Radicals*

An important study interviewed U.S. Olympic champions with over 28 combined gold medals. The results showed that the parents and coaches played a critical role in the development of the athlete. Most importantly, there was little outside pressure to win and an increased emphasis on the psychological development. The emphasis was on the process, not the outcome. Parents stressed the ability to focus, manage their emotions, and remain confident.[14]

However, the goal for many today is for their son or daughter to play at the next level and obtain a college scholarship. More specifically, a Division I full scholarship. If that's the goal, the "why" is skewed.

Professional athletics is not addressed in this book for a reason. These athletes need a ridiculous amount of talent and persistence to play professional sports that few can relate. However, the insanity is that an inordinate amount of parents think professional athletics is achievable and realistic. Recent research reported that twenty-six percent of parents with high-school-age children think that they will play professional sports.[14B] What?! The saddest part of this statistic is someone at some point voiced to these parents that professional athletics was possible. If this is the belief related to professional athletes, what is the impression of receiving a Division I scholarship?

First, the likelihood of playing Division I athletics is slim. The average is between three and six percent of high school athletes will play NCAA athletics, not to mention earn a scholarship. Unless you have a daughter or your son plays either basketball or football, a partial Division I scholarship is likely all that they could procure. The financial commitment to the next level of play may or may not yield a return.[15]

Second, if a scholarship is the motivation for playing there is an expectation for this to be fulfilled. The expectations can lead to overall greater stress, pressure, and more issues such as early specialization, burnout, less creativity, and increased chance of over-use injuries. Once the sacrifice and pressure become greater than the rewards and the enjoyment, athletes begin to quit or switch to another endeavor.

- *Cordell Broadus might be a name you've heard. He was a four-star player recruited by several high-profile Division I schools. He also happened to be rapper Snoop Dogg's son and his journey of playing football was well documented on the television show of A Dad's Dream. Cordell accepted a scholarship to UCLA to play football but quit before his freshman season began.[16]*

- *Becky Dionne was a swimmer since the age of six, and three-time swimmer of the year in New Hampshire. She accepted a scholarship to swim at Savannah College of Art and Design, one of the top schools in the nation for fashion design. After one season, she left the team. She said, "The words 'your scholarship will be pulled' were some of the best I've heard in my life."[17]*

- *Zach McRoberts was a good high school basketball player who committed to the University of Vermont. As a 6'7" forward, he saw action his freshman year and even averaged 7 points and 4 rebounds a game during post-season play. He dropped basketball and transferred after his freshman year because "his heart wasn't in it anymore."[18]*

- *Maggie Teets competed year round in gymnastics since the age of three. After her sophomore year at Stanford University, she made the difficult decision to stop competing. "But coming in and starting, I think I cried every day for months. It was a lot to take in."[19]*

These examples are not necessarily the norm, but they are more common than you might think.

Third, parents often only see the bright shiny diamond of Division I athletics. In some cases, that is the accurate way to go, but Division I athletics are exceptionally demanding. An NCAA survey revealed that a typical athlete in-season spent 39 hours a week on academics and 33 hours per week on their chosen sport. For instance, in Division I basketball alone, approximately forty percent depart their initial school

Don't Should on Your Kids

by the end of their sophomore year. Transfers have become an entire recruiting class essentially.[20]

Parents can get caught up in only the route of Division I that they don't even look for good opportunities at other levels with great educations such as NAIA or Division II schools. Other levels of play can provide athletic-based financial aid, often augmented with academic scholarships.

We've seen parents blind-sided because their son or daughter received a recruiting letter from a Division I university, thinking it was only a matter of time before a scholarship offer would follow. Reality is not best served on a plate of expectations of a Division I scholarship. Vicarious parents ride the wave of recruiting and often use their child's talents as a surfboard, showing them off as their own accomplishments. These actions by parents add to the pressure kids experience.

We see too often individuals with necessary athletic ability to play at the Division I level, but due to poor grades that option was unavailable. Athletics should remain a privilege, not a right. Academics are the true indicator of the options that will remain open for athletes. Academics can also make the biggest difference over an entire lifespan well beyond playing athletics.

If a scholarship is the byproduct and not the driver, then parents can emphasize and reinforce all of the benefits that sport can provide: confidence, motivation, mental toughness, teamwork, communication, and leadership. If a scholarship is a byproduct, then options remain open. These decisions can range from no longer playing in college to examining other avenues of collegiate participation.

The goal is for our child to benefit as a person from the lessons that sport and coaching can provide. There are so many talented athletes at the collegiate level that participating in college needs to be a good fit. There is not a one size fits all. They may be talented enough for a larger program, so is that what your child wants? Some schools are simply better suited for different types of individuals.

A few questions to assess the proper fit of a college:

1. How much do they value winning compared to playing?

2. Can your child earn playing time?

3. How important is a balance between academics and athletics?

4. What is the level of commitment between academics and athletics? *(Every school varies.)*

5. Did they enjoy the feel of the program and underclass members of the team, not just the seniors?

6. How important is proximity to home?

7. If they were injured, would they still want to attend this school for the education?

8. Do they know and understand the communication style of the coach?

Tenacity is More Important Than Talent

Work for a cause, not an applause.

If you watch any collegiate event in basically any sport, you'll witness talent. Talent is through the roof. Bigger, stronger, faster is the proof.[21,22]

- More players than ever before are throwing faster than 90 mph.

- The men's marathon record currently sits at 2:03, which is an average of 4:42 per mile.

- The average lineman in Division I college football is 6'3" and weighs 302 pounds.

- College team golf scores have gotten better by ten strokes per round between the best team and the 60th best team.

All of these improvements are not due solely to God-given genetics. Technology and improvement in training methods have also made a big difference.

David Epstein, the author of *The Sports Gene*, points out that 2012 Usain Bolt's world record-setting the pace in the 100-meter dash bested 1936 winner and world record holder Jesse Owens by 14 feet. However, he goes on to show the technological differences. Jesse Owens ran on cinders and had to use a towel to help dig his feet in at the start. Today's sprinters run on specifically made surfaces with optimal starting blocks. If no technology differences existed, the difference between the two would have only been one stride.[23]

Everyone at the next level has talent. So talent is not the deciding variable. The difference eventually becomes mental toughness: how one responds to adversity and the will to improve. College basketball coach Bobby Knight said, "The will to prepare has to be greater than the will to win."

Coaching motivation is like pushing a rope; it is difficult. Our kids have to want it, they have to initiate, and they need to drive themselves from within.

Our role is to help them foster the tenacity and drive. Tenacity will eventually win out over education and talent. More importantly, tenacity is a skill that transfers outside of sport into life. That's the goal of sport.

Parent Strategy: End Practice Early

There are a few secrets to success: courage, goal setting, and focus. However, one secret that seems to hold true is the ability of "one more." When we are tired and fatigued, the key is to be able to endure just one more. Doing one more rep, writing one more page, making one more sales call, and taking one more step. Just one more. Often, it is effective. There is a prerequisite to implementing this strategy—first we must have the passion and the will or coaching to do one more.

As parents, we have heard and proclaimed this just one more technique. We push, just a little bit (some, unfortunately, push a lot) for our son or daughter to give more effort. Add up the number of practices and seasons of one more and that is a lot of externally driven passion in the form of nagging or strong-arming our son or daughter into practice.

Hall of fame tennis coach Jeff Smith used a different strategy to help build the passion in his son Bryan Smith; he would end practice early. First he would tell Bryan how long they were going to hit tennis balls on the court. It would be either 30 minutes, 45 minutes, or an hour. So, if they were going to hit for 45 minutes, after 20 or 25 minutes he would end the practice and tell Bryan they were ending.

Bryan, having fun, didn't want to end early. So, he would ask his dad to continue. The seed of passion was growing slowly without the nagging, pleading or coercion of "one more." Try out this technique to build motivation. It works.

Reward Effort, Not Rankings or Winnings

Great parents ask their kid, "How was your day?"
not just "How was your practice?"

A father once told us a cute story of how his young 4-year-old daughter began playing golf. As she would ride along in the cart, she noticed people became happy when the ball went in the cup. So, on the next hole, she ran out of the cart, picked up the ball and put it into the cup, raising her hands and waiting for the cheer.

There is nothing wrong with winning—just the emphasis on winning. The applause, pats on the back, and the recognition from winning are infectious. They feel really good. The recognition feels so good that an interesting change occurs. Children actually start to play for the cheers and the recognition that winning brings. Our identity becomes engrossed in the belief that this is how people show appreciation.

Winning, rankings, and trophies cannot be the main emphasis. It's best to stress development, mastery, and effort over other goals. Parents have expressed that their kid at age 13 or 14 is at a crossroads. How can a child be at a crossroad at such a young age unless we are emphasizing the wrong things?

An emphasis only on winning brings pressure to win. The number one reason children quit playing is because it is no longer fun, due to the pressure to win. Sports are fun, allow it to be fun.

The funny thing about sports and life is that we lose more than we win. We will miss more shots, putts, and matches than we will ever connect on. Tiger Woods at his most dominant stretch during the early 2000s won only 25 percent of his tournaments. The top 100 women professional tennis players have a win/loss ratio of only 1.5/1—meaning the best in the world win only a half of a match more than they lose.[24]

Are we concerned mostly with winning, or the lessons that setbacks, adversity, and losing can convey? How do we respond when these occur? Winning doesn't need much of a teacher except how to win with respect. The outside pressure to win is evident. We must avoid the emphasis and discussion with our child.

How many points did you score? What did you shoot? Did you win? Are all questions based on outcome and raise the flag of the importance of winning. Instead, address questions that emphasize effort. *Did you give all of your total effort, and what did you learn?* Ask questions that emphasize the values that matter the most to you.

Ownership, Not Buy-In

Supportive parents build capacity, not dependence.

One of the coolest stories in Mark Twain's *The Adventures of Tom Sawyer* is about the fence. Aunt Polly tasked Tom Sawyer on a sunny day to whitewash the entire fence. What took place is that Tom conveyed to every other kid that came along that he was having fun. He wouldn't let anyone else join in the fun. Only after the kids started pleading and begging did he "allow" others to join in the "fun" and help whitewash the entire fence. He made each person who joined take ownership that it was something they wanted to do.

Some of the first jobs we had were most likely working for someone. A good boss had conversations with us about the company vision, our roles, and possible goals. He or she had us buy in. If things went wrong with the company, we could find another job. Ownership, on the other hand, is much deeper. It means we have a total vested interest in the bottom line, who we hire, and our customers. A good owner must be all in.

Often parents and coaches think of getting athletes to buy in instead of taking ownership. When athletes take ownership of their development, it means that they have skin in the game and stock in the company.

UCLA basketball coach John Wooden stated that the worst punishment he could give would be to withhold practice. The worst punishment was for him to announce, "Gentleman, practice is over." His players took ownership that playing and practicing at UCLA was a privilege and it could be taken away.

Allow your child to take ownership. Ownership builds mental toughness. Let them fail and learn from that failure. Don't try to save the day by not letting them experience the setbacks or the mistakes. Working through the setbacks is a part of learning and growing mentally tough.

Dara Torres, who won twelve Olympic medals in five Olympic Games in swimming, has a strategy for building ownership—she drops her daughter off at practice. It keeps her from getting too involved and allows the coaches to do their job. Athletics can teach whatever we want it to teach, so try allowing the practice to go on without your involvement. Coaches coach, parents parent.

Parent Strategy: I Pack, We Pack, You Pack...

When and if your son or daughter forgets a piece of equipment at home *(glove, Gatorade, jersey, goggles, putter)*, DO NOT PICK IT UP FOR THEM. They will assume ownership in their development and equipment, and they won't forget it again. Interesting how they never seem to forget their hair gel though.

Parents often comment how they get worn out nagging their kids to pack their things and to practice. Who would have thought the task of packing up would become its own sport?

Dan Gould, head of the Institute for the Study of Youth Sports, provides an ownership strategy for athletes. They take ownership of their equipment bag. It's called, "*I pack, we pack, you pack.*"

1. I pack the bag first, and you watch how it's done and observe everything that's needed.

2. Next, we pack the bag together, taking turns, quizzing each other, and making it collaborative.

3. Finally, you pack the bag, and I'll supervise and integrate when and if needed, again, making it fun.

After the last packing, it is completely up to them from that moment on.

It seems such a simple concept so many tasks can be completed with this method. Lastly, allow them ownership to carry their own packed bag.

Don't You Think I'm Trying?

How good do you want to be?

Finding Forrester is a great movie. Jamal Wallace, the main character, is a brilliant mind and a great basketball player. In one of the last scenes of the movie, Jamal (who made 50 consecutive free-throws earlier in the movie) misses two free throws and loses the championship game. What is crucial is the implication that he missed both free throws on purpose.

Parents, I can assure you that your child does not hit a drive out of bounds, miss a shot, throw an interception or race poorly ON PURPOSE!

Yes, they may not always put forth their best effort or their preparation may not be up to the standard it takes, but their mistakes are not punitive at you. Remember, it is not about you.

It's risky to overly question their mistakes as a lack of effort because that line will get old fast. They'll perceive the questions you ask really as accusations: "Why did you, "How could you" and "Are you" type questions. Remember, don't should on your kid. Once they perceive you as constantly accusing them of not giving their best effort, two things can happen:

1. They will shut down and withdraw from you.

2. They will play worse because they become afraid of making mistakes.

There is a solution to this issue. There is an easier, softer way to keep the relationship strong and help them build mental toughness at the same time.

Effort is a non-negotiable when it comes to preparation. Shouldn't we expect that our son or daughter give total effort? This skill will transfer into real life and beyond.

Talk to your children about how good they want to become. Parents often lack the knowledge of what is required for elite status and most

8-year-olds do not have the awareness of what it actually takes to be elite. Allow them to set realistic expectations for the season and receive permission to hold them accountable.

Parent Strategy: I Notice

Parents sometimes struggle with not being able to get through to their kids. Instead of *shoulding* on your kids or asking questions they perceive as challenging their effort or attitude, try a different strategy.

Use the phrase "I notice" instead. James Altucher devised this strategy of "I notice" as a means to look at the situation from a different perspective. For example, instead of "I'm anxious," James says, "I notice I'm feeling anxious." It separates himself from the anxiety.

Instead of saying, "I shouldn't have eaten that piece of cake," try, "I notice I ate the piece of cake." Practicing non-judgmental behavior is better than shaming others or ourselves.

Which of the following statements do you think is better to use?

- You shouldn't be so passive out there; you need to hustle more.

OR

- I noticed you looked a little laid back out there. You seemed like you didn't have much energy.

Make statements of observations instead of pointed commands. Allow them a voice in how they explain themselves and what transpired. The communication stays open and they can internalize the feedback much easier and effectively. When we *should* on our kids, we are making it about our feelings and not their experience. Our role is to be supportive, not vicarious. We aren't supposed to solve their issues or coach, merely provide them opportunities to become mentally tough.

When the Student is Ready, the Teacher Will Appear

*I felt like if I pushed these kids into sports,
I thought that'd backfire on me.*

—Archie Manning

On some of the mini tours in golf, we've heard a similar story from several players who just played a bad round. They'd say, "I hit thirteen greens today [great], hit twelve fairways [great], and thirty-six putts [not good]." After processing, they'd say, "I need to work on my driver." Every outside golf professional and statistician would have had the same question we did. "Thirty-six putts, and it's your *driver?*"

We desire to improve our situation but are unwilling to improve ourselves. If someone has not experienced enough negative outcomes from their actions, then they won't see the need or have the desire to improve. At some point as an athlete, you realize you need to improve. When a child can humbly come to terms with that moment, hopefully, they will address the issue.

When the student is ready, the teacher will appear…

The worst type of advice is unsolicited advice. Just like we would never go up to someone cold and say, "You know what your problem is," we cannot assume an aggressive position when trying to help our own child. They must invite it. The desire must come from them.

As teenagers, Peyton and Eli Manning would go to the football field with their dad to throw and practice. They would watch their 40-year-old father doing 350-yard sprints on the track. As Mr. Manning illustrates, be the model you want your son or daughter to witness.

Asking your son or daughter to practice *with* you is different than telling them to practice for you. It's a difference between a vicarious and supportive parent. Have fun with them; enjoy the times at practice and spending time with one another. Some kids will remain more coachable than others and some will be more iron-willed. Our role is to have them ready to receive the information—even soliciting it themselves.

The skill is to offer feedback, not force feedback. Ask them if they want to discuss their game or strategy. "Just let me know" is a more open and safe approach to creating the atmosphere for growth and confidence building.

Parent Strategy: Permission, Please

Often the best lessons and feedback are ones we don't know we are receiving. Having a discussion about expectations for the upcoming season is healthy, as long it is a conversation and not a mandate.

Ask and gain permission to discuss how your son or daughter will prepare this upcoming season. What kind of goals do they want to set? Encourage them to think about a plan they're comfortable with. Will it be three days a week of making 10 free throws in a row, or maybe one day a week of extra batting practice?

We can operate much better as parents when we know what it is that they want. Then we can ask, "Permission to hold you accountable and support your commitment?"

We want the drive to come from them and they have to want it. When they commit and we've gained their permission, then we can hold them accountable.

We must be able to accept the alternative, however. They may just want to play with their friends recreationally as opposed to tournament play. If this is the case, pulling the plug and shutting down the lessons will be difficult (for you) but necessary. Their passion needs to be present. It may hurt, but we need to scale back our wants and be ready to jump back in and support them, when and if they become ready.

The fear is often that if they don't play at ages 8-10, then they won't be able to play later on at ages 13-15. The solution is to keep active with them and ensuring development still takes place. That way, their options can remain open.

Pre-Game

The pre-game season is also the pre-game period of mental toughness. The theme of pre-game mental toughness is CONFIDENCE.

Less is more during these times. Too often, we err on the complex, heavy side. We try to do too much. We question if our children are prepared or nervous. We nag them about their routine or make it more important than it really is. This section is devoted simply to a few key roles that we can implement to help build their confidence.

Don't Build It Up

Life is a daring adventure or not at all.

—Helen Keller

Olympic diving coach John Wingfield, coach of 2012 gold medalist David Boudia, says there are two types of game-day athletes. He calls them "plus or minus athletes." His theory is based on the research from George Miller. The principle that the average number of information bits we retain in our short-term memory is seven. For example, the length of our phone number.[25]

Plus-two athletes can comprehend more information and perform better when they are aware of all the necessary information. These individuals need the information, yet can be over-thinkers at times.

Minus-two athletes perform worse with added information. These are the "wash and wear" type of competitors. They can handle only three pieces of information at any one time. This type plays better when told very little.

The closer we get to competition and during days of competition, stress levels and cognitive processes automatically increase and the amount of information we can process drops. Some information bits, for example, are what and when to eat, where to park, and is everything packed.

As important competitions get closer, general stress levels increase around the whole family. Athletes start to narrow their focus and small issues can become larger than life.

As parents, we help those around us by not adding undue pressure. However, we tend to want to talk about strategy, competition or other things going on around the team or event.

Pressure mounts the more we discuss and analyze the event and the occasion. It is here you need to comprehend the seven bits principle.

Discuss anything but the upcoming competition. We must understand that this is the process of competing and we can't solve anything for them. Our role is to provide a safe environment free from added pressure.

Recognize that your child's stress level will be high as well. Be aware not to acknowledge any disagreements, squabbles or skirmishes. It doesn't mean to ignore these issues, but merely assign a better time to discuss them.

Information and logistics that need to be discussed prior to the event should take place at least three to five days beforehand. It can then be followed up—but not introduced the day before.

Words of encouragement the day before and on game day are awesome, and again these words spoken should address the process, not the product.

Nervous or Excited?

Know so you can show.

Claire Eccles, 16-year-old rookie pitcher for Canadian Women's National Team, got her start at the Women's Baseball World Cup. She said, "I wasn't [nervous] this time, just extremely excited."[26]

What's the difference between being nervous or excited? It is such a sought-after answer that the question became a huge part of the book, *NO FEAR: A Simple Guide to Mental Toughness.*

Our reaction to stress and pressure physiologically is the same. Our heart races, our minds are full of thoughts, our breathing gets shallow, palms get sweaty, and we even feel the urge to urinate. Back in caveman days, our reaction was a defense mechanism to escape from a predator. Our ancestors responded to this feeling or died.

The difference between getting nervous and excited is our perception and response to our perception. If we perceive events with the expectation that something bad can happen, (I could lose or I don't want to be in the situation), then we will get nervous. On the other hand, if we perceive situations with the expectation that something good could happen, (I could win or I want to be here), then we get excited.

That's the difference!

Parent Strategy: Get Excited

Aren't we actually excited for the tournament rather than anxious? Remove the word nervous from your vocabulary and replace it with excited instead. When the time is close to important events do not ask your child if they are nervous. This doesn't help. Should they be nervous? Not if you don't tell them they should. Avoid even introducing the thought.

Likewise, remember the feeling you have as a parent means you're excited as well, not nervous. Anticipate good things. If you're relaxed, then your child will be more relaxed.

In sports and life, things can go wrong. The game and situation itself will provide enough excitement, so be excited, not nervous. Your role is not to live vicariously through their performance.

Focus on the Process, Not the Product

*An emphasis on winning does not lead
to winning—a focus on the process does.*

A disgusting thing occurs after every national championship in professional sports. After the celebration and speeches, the media ends with an odd question. They ask, "Do you think they will repeat?" This is immediately after a team has won the greatest prize!

Fear emerges from focusing only on the outcome. *Will they make it? Will they earn a partial scholarship? Will they win?* All are rhetorical questions based on the result, the outcome, and the product. There is an unknown to these questions, which brings fear. If fear were a person, it would tell us only to focus on things we cannot control.

Too often, we focus only on winning or losing. To change the atmosphere to positive, focus on and address the process and what they did well, not the outcome of the competition.

It's not what we get from winning; it's who we become. A focus on the process means noticing how we compete, what we do when we play our best, and knowing our own recipe for success. The process is also about who we are becoming, what we excel at, and learn from. The process means addressing effort, teammates, other people excelling, how we handle bad calls, referees, and coaches. These are the lessons and skills that show us how to be successful and that transfer into life.

If we were to dig deeper into this and have the courage to uncover what is bothering us, it is a lack of confidence that the product will turn out how and when we want. We feel anxious and try to put more emphasis on the outcome, only creating more pressure.

Championships are not given away. Not one person would accept a trophy if they did nothing for it. The best athletes shed tears after such championships because they realize how much sacrifice and struggle it took to achieve their goal. It's the journey and the sacrifice that makes it actually mean something.

Call Them This . . .

*Don't let the noise of others' opinions
drown out your own inner voice.*

−Steve Jobs

A study in 2002 from the *Journal of Attitudes and Social Cognition* examined people's names and the impact on careers they chose. The researchers found that people named Dennis were statistically more likely to become dentists. They contended that a phenomenon existed called "implicit egotism." The words that we associate with our names can actually shape our decisions and identity. It doesn't mean that every Lauren becomes a lawyer or every Dennis becomes a dentist, but merely that we gravitate toward the things and names that we associate most with.[28]

"Perfect little Rachel." That's how her parents described and introduced their child, a high-school second baseman. Perfection is a pretty high expectation and I was curious how long they had been calling her that. Unfortunately, she was not mentally tough, and it had little to do with her and more to do with expectations placed on her.

How do you introduce and describe your kids? *"There goes our little winner"* or *"Here comes Johnny, our star goalie."* Be careful about using descriptors that emphasize only part of your child's identity. No one is always a winner and we certainly don't always lose. We are also only an athlete at certain times. These are just things we do—not who we are.

Parent Strategy: Call Them a Competitor!

We can compete in everything we do. We can compete in grades, paying attention, and playing sports. However, too much of competition involves beating or besting someone else. To define it in a healthy way for your child, emphasize that competition means against yourself, not anyone else. In this way you will be teaching your child not to compare themselves to others, which often results in low self-esteem. Teach them to have an audience of one and that is the only one that matters.

In The Game

In-game is where it all comes out. Everything that's been going on behind the scenes is now up front for everyone to see. During the game is when so many parents are criticized. Coaches remark that the kids haven't changed as much as the parents have throughout the years. Frankly, we have no idea what happens behind closed doors inside of someone's home. We don't know if they push their kid or if they criticize effort. However, we can and do witness their behavior at the games and on the field. Parental behavior on the field not only affects your own children but anyone else in earshot.

To create in-game mental toughness, our focus should be on modeling. Our goal is to model the behavior that we want to see in our own children. If an outsider were to watch only the parents' behavior during competition, they would be able to tell from that which athletes are relaxed and which ones are stressed. Parents model the behavior and kids follow it. Parents that are relaxed and not stressed during games produce athletes of like mind.

We can do more harm than good during these times. The toughest part is that we want it so bad for them, but it is out of our control; we can't do anything about their performance. It is at this crucial time during the game that our behavior is most influential—and where the most harm can be done.

The Lion's Den

Did you think the lion was sleeping because he didn't roar?

—*Friedrich Schiller*

There is an energy to sports. One of the coolest feelings is that electricity of an important game or match. Electricity can cause shocks, however, and it only takes one charge for the current to get started.

The lion's den is the area where all the parents congregate during the game.

This area is usually the bleachers, but it varies depending on the sport. The lion's den can be a very happy or downright scary place. During the happy times, the lions are playful with one another. Everyone is cheering, joking around, and discussing the local culture.

However, it takes only one negative play or person for the lion's den to roar. It's like the pack spotted a gazelle and they start to froth at the mouth.

Here's how it often transpires: One person yells at their kid to grab a rebound or hustle or jeers the team for running a certain play or not executing. Once a ref makes a questionable call, all of the parents are now in complete unison. The electricity is now directed as a collective unit toward a ref or an opposing player. Once the cheering turns into shouting, the lion's den is complete. They are ready to devour anyone that crosses them.

It's almost impossible to control emotions in the lion's den because the energy and environment are so emotionally charged. Many of the transgressions and ill-fated reactions throughout history from negative parents have occurred directly within the lion's den. You would be wise to check yourself in this situation that you do not get caught up in the mob mentality and pounce on anyone.

Parent Strategy: The Blow Pop

Umpires possess the toughest position on the field and are discussed only when something bad happens. However, one little league umpire came up with a genius way to settle down the lion's den of parents. He was finished with all of the loud parents who would criticize their son and daughter when they played. Since umpires are not a favorite type of person, anytime this guy approached the crowd to settle down boisterous parents, it rarely went well. So, he devised a strategy with an action that spoke louder than any words.

He started taking Charms Blow Pops with him to the game and told the coaches at every game what he was going to do. When a parent would become too loud and criticize their son or daughter, he would have the Blow Pop delivered to the parent with no explanation. No words were spoken. Many of the parents would just enjoy the Blow Pop. Immediately they quieted down, and they got the message quickly. Blow Pops meant shut it up. It worked!

You Can Communicate Too Much

You "can't" communicate too much with your team.

—Coach John Groce

During a youth hockey game, a 12-year-old crossed the blue line with the puck. From the stands, his dad yelled, "Shoot it!" The 12-year-old froze! That voice was stuck inside his head for the entire season. He was a great passer at that age but had not yet developed a strong slap shot. One critical shout from his dad and he now began to have doubts and think instead of just play.

There are good opportunities to talk about their performance—and some not good ones. During the game is NOT a good time to bring it up. However, we constantly see parents communicating with their son or daughter while they are playing.

A strange thing occurs when a parent regularly provides instructions or feedback while a young athlete plays—the athlete hears it! There can be hundreds of people in the stands and a young athlete will single out a parent's voice. Since your voice is the one they've heard their whole life, they can't block it out.

The above quote by John Groce seems contradictory to the section title, but there is a difference between a coach and a parent. Sport requires focus and the one voice they should be listening to is the coach. Athletes at all levels mention that when they feel they have conflicting coaches, they are less likely to play well. They want to do what the coach demands, but also please their parents at the same time.

Cheer and be positive during games and especially for other teammates, but avoid feedback or coaching while your son or daughter is playing the game. There may be a time and place for that—but it's not here and not now.

Parent Strategy: Have a Plan

We didn't plan to fail; we just failed to plan. Often we didn't mean to yell or scream or lose it in the stands. We just allowed our emotions to take over. The game cannot turn into an occasion for that. As parents, we must have a plan as to how we will conduct ourselves and how we will cheer.

Make an agreement with yourself and son or daughter about how you'll act and cheer. This agreement with ourselves must take place before we arrive. Again, root for others on the team, not just your child.

Body Language Doesn't Talk, It Screams

Sometimes it swears.

Question: In which sport do you think body language is the most crucial?

Yes, all of them, but more so in gymnastics. They not only have incredible athleticism, but they must always smile at the end of their performance. Smiling to the judges is crucial even after a poor routine or dismount, although it might be the last thing they want to do. A gymnast's smile is either extremely genuine or extremely fake.

In all sports, we see positive and negative body language on the field. As parents, our body language off the field speaks so loud your son or daughter doesn't need to hear a word you're saying. They can see you slump, get upset or throw your hands up in disgust. I repeat—they can see your negative body language.

This is not easy, but it is essential—your own body language must remain confident and supportive. That means your head is always up, you are clapping or cheering, and giving thumbs up.

When things are not going as well as we'd like, we must immediately focus on our own body language and what it is communicating. Why?

Negative body language doesn't show that you care or are passionate; it reveals a lack of confidence. Things are going to go wrong, our kids will face adversity, and people will make mistakes. If we lose our cool and show horrible reactions to events, then what are we really saying?

When our body language is negative, we are demonstrating and showing that we don't think the result is going to turn out like we'd hoped. We don't have confidence or faith in our child.

I am not an advocate of faking it until we make it, because then we are just faking it. I merely say act as if. Act as if they will turn it around and finish strong.

Great parents demonstrate confident body language.

Respond, Don't React

"Do you have the patience to wait till the mud settles and the water is clear?"

—Lao Tzu

In the book, *NO FEAR: A Simple Guide to Mental Toughness*, the concept of respond, don't react was a huge component of mental toughness.[27]

Think of a reactor and you get a vision of a nuclear power plant or a chemical bond. A reactor is someone who can't keep his or her cool under pressure. Picture a responder on the other hand, and you get a first responder, someone who has been trained to handle adversity.

We need to be a responder with our athletes, not a reactor. When we respond, it is devoid of emotion and we usually make good decisions. It is operating from a place of calmness and reason. When we react, however, it is full of emotion and knee-jerk behaviors. Many careers and mistakes have occurred due to a bad reaction.

Parent Strategy: What Your Kid Really Wants to Hear

Baseball coach Adam Wiginton from Kansas implemented a new strategy. Before the first parent meeting of the season, he asked his players to anonymously write out how they wanted their parents to act at the game. He felt that having his players' voices heard was key to changing the behavior of parents.

Some of the responses by his players included:

"Don't talk to me on the mound."

"Don't talk to me in the on-deck circle."

"Don't yell at umps; it's just embarrassing."

"Don't criticize coach's decision or tell me what he should have done."

At the parent meeting, Wiginton shared all of the responses and made the parents aware that this is their son speaking directly to them. I'm sure it stung a bit, but as a result of the proactive approach, the result was the best year ever.

Post-Game

Some text messages a coach or player receives after a national championship win can range in the hundreds to the thousands, not to mention the number of mentions on Twitter. How many messages does a coach or player receive after a similar loss? Depending on how the game was lost, not many.

Winning is usually not as difficult to deal with unless we are that parent who manages to criticize why they weren't perfect. Losing is where the pain resides. Not just losing the game—this can be over losing playing time, a bad play or the big loss. We should see the bigger picture that we are all going to lose more than we are ever going to win. Developing a plan on how to handle losing and keeping it in perspective is an important life skill.

The post-game and even post-practice can be raw. After the game is when players question their "why." Why am I out here? Why do I keep playing? Why are others getting more praise?

Mental toughness can be greatly enhanced when the post-game is handled correctly. Conversely, mental toughness can take a big hit if post-games are not handled correctly.

Ride the Carousel, Not the Roller Coaster

Success has a thousand fathers. Failure is an orphan.

A caddy on the PGA tour is the closest experience to being a sideline coach. Besides walking with and helping them, you're the only person who can give them advice during the round.

On the PGA tour, the golfer's name is on the bag for a reason—they are the one hitting the shots. However, there is a common saying among caddies. When their golfer plays well, they say, "*We* shot sixty-seven." If their golfer does not play well, they say, "*He* shot seventy-four."

It is difficult being a caddy, though, when your player makes a mistake, bogies or misses a cut. The margin between success and failure is so slim and a caddie's income depends on how the player performs. One can easily get fixed up in the emotion and disappointment that a player feels when playing poorly. Great caddies have that bond and rapport down pat. They simply know what their player thinks before he or she says anything.

Great caddies remain emotionally unattached from poor outcomes. Parenting is the same way. As a caddy and parent, we cannot ride the emotional roller coaster that our competitor will feel during a game or season. When we do, it means that we've become vicarious parents and are living and dying on every play.

Our role is to be supportive. That means we must stay emotionally stable and available. When players struggle, they need a supportive, non-judgmental environment. Also, if and when they ask us for advice or suggestions, we need to be there for them.

If we have been riding the roller coaster of ups and downs, then we cannot be unbiased and level-headed like we should be. The carousel is not as fun to ride, but as for how we parent, it's the best ride we can take.

The Car Ride

Great caddying is all about timing.

—JOE SKOVRON

During his junior season in college, this discus and hammer thrower was having a good season. However, during NCAA regionals, he had his worst meet of the season and did not qualify for nationals. His parents were at the meet and he decided to spend a few minutes after his poor performance talking with them. Even though the season was over his coach wanted to discuss what he did wrong at that exact moment, interrupting his family time. Let's just say, that the interaction between coach and athlete went less than favorable.

Coaching is all about timing.

We have all been there: Our son or daughter not only played poorly, but played with little energy, couldn't let go of mistakes, and they may even have looked like they didn't want to be there.

Since we value effort and it wasn't there, we took mental notes on what we were going to say and how to best get our point across. We wanted to make sure that history does not repeat itself.

Parenting is all about timing.

There are good times to talk with your son or daughter about the game, and then there are bad times. *On the ride home from the game and practice is a bad time.*

Worth repeating: The worst time to discuss" performance is on the ride home. We may want to talk so bad that it is like acid in our mouth—they need to know what we think. We have great points, and they need to know how they can improve. All true, but we just cannot share them on the ride home.

Even if we commend and not criticize, we may get in the habit of making the car ride *the time* and *place* to discuss. They are trapped in the confines and have to listen. When athletes play poorly, the last thing they want to hear is someone trying to make them feel better. In fact, it doesn't help build their mental toughness because they need to feel the pain of not getting what they want.

Parent Strategy: The Talk

Sadly, many parents have an over-reliance of using text messaging to communicate important thoughts and sensitive subjects. Communicating the game or practice via text is not the best medium because too much gets lost in translation. It's impossible to effectively listen to or share personal thoughts. Remember, it's not what you say; it's what they hear. Sending a 300-word text may be perceived as shouting or *shoulding* on them, and in return, you'll receive a one-word reply. If you find yourself upset because "we don't talk anymore," evaluate your use of text messaging. Set the example of how effective in-person communication should take place. For in-depth conversations, one text is too many and a thousand is never enough.

Try setting up an agreed-upon time for an in-person discussion about the game or practice. This might be after dinner or after cleaning up or even the next day—whatever you agree upon as a family. Your child will appreciate the time to decompress and not dread the car ride home like their friends who get grilled every time.

So much can be accomplished after we are cool, calm, and collected. And especially after your child is calm and given time to process.

Resist the urge to talk more than listen. Allow them to provide the feedback about what they did well and what they learned from their play. They take much more ownership when they are doing the talking.

Lastly, as coach Brett Hawke said, "catch them doing it right."

Cover Your Answers

Let them figure it out.

We were in the office of a Division I basketball team during a pre-season meeting. The outstanding group of staff and coaches approach the game the right way. On this particular morning, the head coach and his two assistants were going over the "pick and roll" offensive play at length.

After five minutes, it was like learning Spanish and then trying to follow a conversation between three very fluent speakers. No one understood what was going on. Here's the key—as coaches, sports are our profession and we are compensated very well to know the intricacies of all sports. However, this level of explanation and description between the three coaches went six levels deep, and fast!

A successful collegiate coach recently said, "I wish they wouldn't keep asking, 'What am I doing wrong?' all the time! I want them to find a way, battle, and make adjustments."

If we want to know why kids feel entitled to playing time, winning, and success, then you may particularly enjoy the following. What's changed is that kids no longer have to "figure it out." They don't have to remain uncomfortable or find a way. Nowadays, when athletes struggle, someone else provides the answer sheet. We take care of it and taking care of it doesn't build mental toughness, it builds entitlement.

On a micro-level, when players are struggling for answers, they can just look it up on the Internet or ask someone to fix it. "Fix my technique" often becomes a battle cry. The answers are very accessible and affordable. If they don't like the answer, then they can ask someone else. Also, they don't have to wait for anything; the patience of having to figure things out only adds stress.

A recent study revealed that we utilize the Internet for so much information that we think we are smarter than we really are. Participants in the study were asked a series of questions in which one group had to think of the answer and the other group was allowed to use Google to find the answer. The research showed that people who merely searched the Internet had an inflated sense of intelligence. The authors concluded that there is a distinct line between what we know and what we think we know.[29]

We are unaware of what takes place in our mind if we are in a social gathering and someone asks the question, "Where was Woodstock held?" or "Who has the Super Bowl single game rushing record?" It actually rarely happens because we don't ask—we just look it up so we won't look silly.

It's like we have morphed into Alex Trebek on Jeopardy! We appear that we have it all together and know the answer. Yes, Mr. Trebek is intelligent, but if we had every answer in front of us, we would appear to be the smartest person on the planet as well.

Personally, searching our own mind and getting uncomfortable with not knowing the answer is a good thing. It causes us to figure it out, find a way, and utilize our mind. That's mental toughness. Isn't it more satisfying when we suddenly realize that Woodstock was at Yasgur's farm or the Super Bowl rushing record was Timmy Smith?

It seems every profession allows us to retake the test as many times as we want: the BAR exam, MCAT, SAT, ACT, and even a driver's test. We don't have an issue with this approach, because it does reward persistence. However, it has become the norm, not the exception and the entitlement spreads. Yes, the person who finishes last in their class is still an M.D., but I don't want that surgeon. There's little accountability or even incentive to handle adversity. Instead, we remove the struggle.

The system has perpetuated the issue. Since we've been providing the answers, why are we shocked when our children expect entitlement? It occurred every step along the path because we removed the learning experience of failing.

Not knowing the solution is painful and uncomfortable. However, the only way to build mental toughness and improve is to find a way, figure it out, and make adjustments. Athletics is one of the last bastions of having to find a way and figure it out, because unlike the test examples above, an athlete's test is the game. Unfortunately, many parents have tried to remove those painful experiences of failing as well.

Let Them Fail

*People have no idea how many times you have
to finish second, in order to finish first.*

— JACK NICKLAUS

It really hurts when we lose and fail. It is no fun at all. There is major discomfort. Even though it hurts, losing is never fatal. But most of us have to go through that experience to figure that part out. Mental toughness is often caught rather than taught.

The big loss is the most difficult. We've unfortunately been in the locker room after the big loss that ended a season—teams and athletes that were confident, yet lost. Anger and sadness accompany the big loss, but the main feeling inside is numbness, the lack of any feeling. If you're in sport and life long enough, you'll experience it.

These losses camouflage as learning lessons. Learning experiences hurt. When we don't win, we learn. That's the path to growth and success.

Losing and failing is challenging, not a tragedy. The pain eventually subsides, but many have removed the setbacks, adversity, and ownership of failing. As a result, we have cheapened the joy of success and winning. We cannot truly appreciate winning and improvement if we have never lost. When we eliminate the pain of losing, we also eliminate the lesson.

Parents remove the pain of teachable moments by blaming coaches, other players or changing teams. If parents do this, they are trying to save the day, but in reality they are not teaching the right lesson. Instead of working on improving our weaknesses and shortcomings, we teach that mom or dad will take care of it.

We must allow our athletes to experience the natural setbacks and struggles, and learn how to overcome these obstacles. They cannot improve if we remove the obstacles. Worse yet, they don't learn how to effectively deal and cope with losing. We cannot remove the natural setbacks and teachable moments that occur at this level.

When our children lose, it's important to let them take ownership and not allow them to blame others. Losing isn't fatal—it just stings a lot. Proper perspective is important. At the right time, ask good questions: What did they learn from it? What do they need to improve upon?

Losing is tough, so allowing them to take ownership does not mean piling on with criticism or critique. We are all vulnerable to a loss, so they still need encouragement, love, and support. As we can't let a win go to our head, we can't allow a loss to go to our heart. They need reassurance after losing that they are still great.

We cannot give away something that we don't have. To provide proper perspective, we must have perspective ourselves. Losing does not make you a bad parent, and winning does not make you a great parent. This experience is about them; it's not about you.

We emphasize winning over development way too much. Kids are focused on having fun, the way they should be. Winning should be the byproduct and its internal reward. Did we just *should* on you again?

We Don't Keep Score, But We Are Up 8-4

"They don't give trophies away...wait, yes, they do."

Trophies by themselves are not bad. Trophies actually don't mean anything. Many Olympians have their gold medals in a sock drawer. We give meaning to the trophy and what it represents. The belief behind trophies is that kids be recognized for participating and showing up. Every participant is awarded a trophy. We've implemented our adult viewpoint on youth sports.

Olympians didn't participate for a medal; it was not the driver. They wanted to test themselves against the best. Their mental toughness and talent are the reasons for their success. I doubt if even one kid ever began to play sports because they thought, "Hey, I get a trophy at the end." They play for the fun and the Capri Sun. When we give kids trophies for participating, it is more about the adults than it is the kids.

The belief of participation trophies is that it will help inspire, motivate, and keep kids coming back. Or perhaps later on our kids can look at their dresser and get a sense of accomplishment from their participation trophy?

However, awarding participation trophies may do more harm than good. We think that providing an external reward for hard work will build motivation, but the opposite may be the case. It may diminish their motivation.

Yale researcher Amy Wrzesniewski examined the motives of over 11,000 West Point cadets across the span of 14 years. They wanted to assess the impact of cadets reason for entering the academy. Cadets that had internal motivators were more likely to graduate, receive promotions, commissions, and stay in the military. Cadets that entered with both strong internal and external motivators (*such as get a good job later in life*) revealed drastically less success. Amazingly, external factors such as get a better job and make more money had a negative impact on overall success.[30]

We all have different internal motivators and are more likely to accomplish a task when we tap into our own "why" rather than a carrot or stick approach. (*Such as returning a wallet because it's the right thing to do, rather than the possible reward I could get.*)

Adults don't need to give trophies to kids for participating; they just need to praise their effort and allow them to have fun and also fail. Have a year-end banquet and provide everyone a ribbon or certificate but just realize that we don't create motivation or make everyone a winner by making everyone not a loser. It may even create more losers.

There is a line of demarcation in athletics when winning eventually trumps development. We are not exactly sure when this occurs, but it's usually when coaches are hired and fired based on performance. When we value winning we stop giving trophies away, and they start earning them.

Don't Go Back to the Cook

A coach is somebody who takes you somewhere you want to go.

—Martin Rooney

A head football coach said, *"I've eaten out at restaurants my entire life and never have I once gone back to the kitchen to tell the cook, this is how you should prepare the meal."* In sports, however, we seem to think that because we can visibly see what takes place on the field, it makes us somewhat of an expert. Coaches devote their time, energy, and expertise to the passion. It's their livelihood to know the nuances and personnel of preparation and execution. Frankly, it's their job to know more than you! Even at the recreational level, they have devoted time.

As parents, we must accept that our perception is skewed because of our emotional investment. To illustrate, imagine you are at a youth football game and the quarterback just throws his second consecutive interception. Do you boo and criticize the kid who threw the ball? Probably not, because this is youth football. So after our initial reaction, we don't boo. But, we are still upset and the anger has to go somewhere. So we say something like, *"Why does coach keep calling so many pass plays?"*

Simply put, there are going to be good and not so good coaches. And our kids learn from both. They learn the healthy way to treat others, and how to communicate, and also, unfortunately, the unhealthy ways. But, kids need to be free to form their own opinions and experience situations without our coloring their perceptions.

Criticizing coaches' play calling, schemes or playing time does much harm to a situation. Coaching from the stands is horrendous.[31] A youth coach once stated that he knows when parents are talking about him behind his back. "The kids won't look me in the eye." Sad.

The lessons learned in sport can transfer out of sport. There are going to be good bosses and not so good bosses. If we wouldn't call up our child's boss ourselves, then why would we call the coach? If there is an issue that your son or daughter needs to communicate with coach, they should be the one communicating.

Mike Lingenfelter is director of Munciana volleyball, a nationally ranked program. He knows coaching. One of his young daughters had a particularly rough season with a basketball coach. At the end of the season, Mike met with the coach. He simply thanked the coach for his time that he devoted to the team. His wife, a bit confused, asked how he could actually thank the coach when they felt he did a poor job?

Lingenfelter understood that coaches make a sacrifice of time away from their own family, no matter the quality of their craft. He thanked the coach for his time, not for his coaching style, and that was all that needed to be said.

Coaches are an important part of our society. Anyone can count shots, laps or drills, but as coach Robert Taylor states, "we don't count reps, we coach reps." We can remember the coach who made an impact in our lives and became a hinge. The great coach that either made a deep and profound impact in our life or even the bad coach that showed us how not to operate or communicate.

Everyone can use a coach.

Unfortunately, coaches at large have stopped receiving their due appreciation. The opposite has occurred; they have become a lightning rod for parents. Parents complain, yell, and even write anonymous emails to the coaches themselves, administration or other parents. Coaches are pestered with questions focused on playing time such as "why didn't my kid start, or play more." Worse, coaches are questioned about other kids performance or strategy, for instance, "why is he/she playing," and "why did you do that play?"

Coaches at all levels sacrifice their time. If you don't coach, then you are awarded more freedom to finish your own business without having to show up early and leave late. It's your choice, we don't judge. But, if you do not step up to coach, you have forfeited your right to sit down and coach.

Parent Strategy: Thank the Cook

Coaches Mark James and Brian Satterfield end practice the same way, they shake each player's hand. Simple, yet powerful. No matter the type of practice or outcome of game, the ending is the same. It was created as a way to put a type of positive closure on a poor day, a way to end it positively. It takes more mental toughness to lift up one's head than it does to raise a trophy.

Players even started looking forward to the handshake. The worst punishment coach could ever deliver is telling one of their players, "I don't want to see you after practice." They would get it together pretty quick.

A positive ending is essential because we can't know the last time we are ever going to see someone. Travis Smith was a freshman golfer in college and we never had another chance to say goodbye after practice. He died in a car accident that weekend. His parents would have given anything to spend just a few more moments with him.

Money isn't the most precious resource, its time. End everything with a handshake and a thank you.

True Success

True success means rooting for everyone.

Duke Basketball fans have one of the most indelible student sections in all of the sports: the Cameron Crazies. They are beyond passionate camping out in Krzyzewskiville for three months prior to games. They are organized and witty, handing out cheat sheets for the student cheers and even coined the now famous "air-ball" chant.

Can you imagine that they once actually cheered for an opposing rival's player? During one game in 1995, Joe Smith of Maryland was unstoppable. He scored forty points against them, had eighteen rebounds, and had a tip-in basket as time expired to beat Duke, 94-92.[32] At the end of the game, after Duke lost, they applauded Joe Smith.

RFK Stadium in Washington, D.C. was considered one of the toughest places in the NFL for away teams to play. The stadium swayed with excitement from the crowd and the Washington fans were some of the most spirited. During a game in 1986 against the New York Giants, Coach Bill Parcells approached his quarterback Phil Simms and told him, *"They hate us so much that they like us."*

True success is being able to root for everyone.

It doesn't mean that we cheer or root for our direct competition. When I post this philosophy on-line, I'll get questions like, "Even the Yankees?"

When we root for others, it means that we are confident. Rooting for everyone means wanting to beat people at their best. It is honoring them for their talent and respecting them as fellow athletes. We should want them to play well, but just for us to play a little bit better. It doesn't take away from our drive or our hating to lose, but we need others to succeed so we know what we have to do to improve.

During the 2015 NBA Finals between the Cleveland Cavaliers and the Golden State Warriors, Kyrie Irving of the Cavaliers re-injured his knee. Steve Kerr, the head coach of the Warriors said, "I hope he can play the rest of the series. You probably don't believe me, but I mean that."[33]

Usually, though, we do the opposite. When others are successful, we are often threatened. Success reminds us of our shortcomings or as Bette Midler said, "the toughest part of success is trying to find others who are happy for you." Conflict between team members is based on the belief that success is limited. Therefore, not only do I need to be the best that I can be, but remove any obstacle in that path, including teammates vying for my position or record.

Parents, unfortunately, perpetuate this notion and encourage this culture as well. Whenever we call out or put down a coach or another child on the team, we are doing so based out of fear and insecurity. The child internalizes these discussions toward other players or coaches, and it teaches them the wrong thing—that it's okay to put others down.

The imaginary lines between towns and teams are witness to these conflicts as well. We spend so much time hating on the success of others that we lose all proportion and focus of improving our own game.

Great sports parents are confident enough in themselves to root for others and show the strength in lifting others up.

Off-Season

This time of the year has significantly been reduced because many fear any off-season. "No off-season" has also been romanticized in today's culture as a badge of honor. Frankly, an off-season is needed from a primary sport. Back when everyone still played multiple sports, there were other sports to play and the transition and break happened naturally. However, now the pressure to play only one sport does not allow for other sports at all.

Kids need rest and disengagement from their sport. The physical side is a huge part of the recovery, but more so is the need for emotional and psychological rest. Competing is stressful and going through mini-slumps and struggle is stressful. The main reason kids stop playing sports is because it is no longer fun. How much mental energy does it take to play five tournaments in a row?

The off-season is the time of year for honest reflection and assessment and time to de-stress and decompress. Encourage your child to stay active and participate in average kid activities. As Dr. Bernice Sorensen said, "a lost childhood is one of the greatest difficulties anyone has to overcome in adulthood."

I Love My Multi-Sport Athletes

Be the coach you wish you had.

—Martin Rooney

Bison once roamed North America and met the food needs of an entire population of indigenous people. Eventually, it was hunted merely for its hide and almost became extinct. Once as many as 60 million bison roamed the plains but in the 1900s that number was reduced to only 300. Thankfully, the numbers have returned to over 400,000.[34]

Like the bison, the multi-sport athlete has slowly been killed off. Playing multiple sports was once revered for the benefits it offered: fun, teamwork, creativity, self-governing, motivation, fitness, and confidence. However, lost somewhere between adolescence and puberty is the specialist, an athlete whose sole purpose is to try and excel at one sport.

The difference between the bison and the multi-sport athlete, however, is that humans could never domesticate the American Bison. We've been able to contain the multi-sport athlete under the guise of falling behind or getting hurt if they don't stick with it.

The latter, "You'll get hurt," is a major misnomer that has been shown to have the opposite effect. *Athletes who specialize have a greater rate of injury compared to non-specialized athletes.* John Smoltz was the first pitcher drafted in the hall of fame who had Tommy John surgery, a surgical procedure commonly prescribed due to overuse injury. Now, almost as many adolescents as professionals are having Tommy John surgery.[35]

"You'll get left out" is the true bison in the room.

The sports skills transfer. Eighty-seven percent of the draft picks in the 2015 NFL draft were multi-sport athletes. This isn't a one-year anomaly either. The average hovers around *70 percent.* All athletic movements transfer—quickness, running, jumping, agility, throwing. For example, the athletic movement of jumping for a basketball is similar and builds the same muscles needed to push off the blocks in swimming and have a good kick.[36]

Indian Wells Tennis Garden in California holds some of the best tennis tournaments every year. Next to the tennis stadium is a massive soccer field. You'll often see many European professional tennis players also playing soccer during tournament downtime. They are multi-sport athletes.

Multi-sport athletes have a greater sport I.Q. They develop a feel for any game they are playing. They are more creative and less mechanical in their approach. They look and move athletically. Conversely, a recent phenomenon in volleyball is that some players in college have never served a ball in competition, ever. There are now specialists inside of specialized athletes.

Multi-sport athletes learn to compete. Each sport is different and requires different levels of focus and resiliency. To become mentally tough, they need to be in different sports situations that test their resilience and ability to make a comeback. If they learn to compete early on, that skill will transfer into other areas as well. They'll be able to compete in anything.

Another benefit—burnout becomes less frequent in multi-sport athletes. How long do you think going to five showcase events and traveling each weekend in the summer to play remains fun? Trust me, once every single tournament becomes a *must do*, the fewer tournaments are. Keep your child's passion and fun alive by allowing breaks and time off.

- Elena Delle Donne was the top basketball recruit in the nation. However, she suffered from burnout and played volleyball her first year in college.

- Marcelo Chierighini was SEC swimmer of the year at Auburn University, a national champion, and Olympian; he didn't start swimming until age 16.

- Andy Roddick played high-school basketball for four years along with tennis.

- Dara Torres, the only U.S. swimmer to swim in five Olympic games, lettered in volleyball during her fifth year of eligibility at the University of Florida.

- Steve Nash played soccer, rugby, and basketball in high school.

- Pat McAfee, the punter in the NFL, played soccer at West Virginia University.

- Maverick McNealy, the top-ranked amateur golfer in the United States while at Stanford University, played hockey, soccer, and golf into his senior year at high school.
- NBA Hall of Famer Tim Duncan was a competitive swimmer who had goals of making the Olympic team.

Multi-sport athletes are better teammates. For example, if your son or daughter plays an individual sport as their primary, they can still garner all the benefits of teamwork in a team sport.

In college, all sports in one way or another are team sports. However, parents and even coaches tend to stress the opposite, coercing kids to specialize too early so they can improve, thereby bypassing the entire team concept in sports. High school sports in general are also going the way of the bison. If your son or daughter plays an individual sport as their primary, they can still garner all the benefits of teamwork in a team sport. Don't discount team play but instead encourage it. As Notre Dame Softball Head Coach Deanna Gumpf says when recruiting, "I love my multi-sport athletes."

What can be learned from playing different sports can be applied to the primary sport. The grit, tenacity, and will to compete are the traits that transfer across all sports.

A final point: The single-sport athlete isn't the worst culprit. It's the multi-sport specialist, the individual who plays on three or four teams for one sport. They specialize early for exposure, meaning they bounce around several different elite travel teams every year. This is the new wave of overlapping specialized sports, where an athlete spreads himself thin but keeps it within the single game.

Where is the time to play unorganized games? Remember fun?

Are You Quitting or Switching?

*Persistence means you get one percent better every day,
no matter how you add it up.*

—JAMES ALTUCHER

At the end of the Cold War the United States remained the lone superpower, but somewhere along the way adopted the old East German approach to sporting development. The best athletes were selected and sent to athletic boarding schools to develop their sporting skills. In China, children are tested on athletic qualities from ages 8 to 13. Flexible children are sent to diving and gymnastics camps, quick reflexes are sent to Ping-Pong, short-arms are guided to weight-lifting and so on.

Currently, systems are in place where if a child shows any level of talent, they are celebrated and elevated. They are encouraged to year-round training and playing. The *next level* verbiage gets tossed around.

Now, if they have a passion for it, by all means, go for it. However, if a child falls out of love or does not enjoy a sport, we must allow them an out. It's best to know the difference between switching sports and quitting.

Speaking with parents of elite U.S. divers, the question was asked, "Should we allow them to quit?" Our answer was YES! Now, we did cringe a little bit even as we said it, and the parent seemed disgusted at our response. Her daughter was probably in the room. Our response was based on the premise that the passion and love must be there, and no child can be forced to love a sport. It's challenging to get better at something if it is no longer fun. Many athletes have taken breaks from their sport to rediscover their passion and their why later on. Mental toughness is more often caught than it is taught.

One of the backbones to success is that to never give up. It was the first point in the book, *NO FEAR: A Simple Guide to Mental Toughness.*

The switching or quitting choice that many athletes face does not fall into the category of never giving up vs. giving up. Quitting and blaming have become more common in today's culture rather than perseverance and responsibility. That is also one of the goals that sport can provide. However, there is a lot more gray area to this situation, so it's best not to be so black and white.

Quitting involves dropping out and not wanting to go through the struggle that is inherent in the sport though the love is still there. Our role is to remain supportive and provide perspective to help see them through.

Switching involves taking a break from a bad situation. It's important to see the distinction and to know which your child is going through so that you can help them work through the decision to their best advantage.

The difference between switching and quitting may even take place in college. Blair Socci played volleyball at UCLA, became a starter, and made the elite eight her freshman year. Unfortunately, Blair hurt her knee at the beginning of her sophomore season. She didn't travel that season and quit the team after Christmas break after the team made the Final Four.

Or did she switch?

Blair wrote that she had "The newfound freedom to reinvent myself...I was invigorated and strangely at peace." She switched from playing volleyball at the highest level to channeling her focus into other things that she never had time before, including writing. When those around her tried to talk her out of it, she never regretted the decision and didn't look back. If it weren't for her injury and switching away from sport, she wouldn't have become a successful comedian and writer.[37]

Mentioning Money and Time

Commend, don't criticize.

"We are paying how much for lessons, and you play this way?"

"We've invested too much time to have you quit."

"This has to pay off."

"Boy, we sure have been doing this a long time."

"You'll take care of your momma one day."

Are these comments intended to increase motivation or pull rank as a parent?

Not all sports are created equal. You are probably already aware of the costs of participating. Depending on where you live, what sport your child plays, and what summer camps they attend, you may pay upwards of $4,000 to $10,000 each year, maybe more. These don't include costs incurred to attend tournaments.[38]

Research on scholarships of Division I athletes shows that behavior of a coach is most important for motivation. Motivation increased or decreased on how the scholarship was communicated to them. If a coach communicated the scholarship as informational (*you're good enough*), then motivation increased. However, if a coach used the scholarship as controlling (*you'll do this because you're on scholarship*), motivation decreased.[39]

The perception of money and time is what is crucial. If it is seen as a tool of information, it will increase motivation. If it is viewed as controlling, then motivation can wane.

As a parent, the role is to be supportive, not controlling. When money or time or the amount of sacrifice that you have made is brought up, it adds pressure. Students and athletes today are in the know; they are aware of cost and sacrifices. Due to the sacrifices made by parents, they often internalize their play and struggle as letting others down.

Discuss all pressure and uncomfortable topics in non-pressure and comfortable environments. Discussing money, time, and financial independence are essential. There is a place to discuss money and time. Communicating and planning from both ends are best discussed before and after every season, certainly not during the season or after bad outcomes.

The financial commitment can be expensive. If college is the goal, then the optimal situation is that money and resources have been invested wisely. Outside of the sports investment that may or may not pay off, financial security in terms of 529 savings or other investment options are advisable. Visit your financial planner or fiduciary to account for a plan B to pay for college rather than relying solely on athletic scholarships.

Parent Strategy: Soft Questions vs. Hard Questions

Basketball coach Jeff Van Gundy once stated, "talk about all pressure decisions and moments in non-pressure environments." His team and staff needed to communicate and be on the same page way before the game began. There needed to be no ambiguity on what play or who was going to take shots in certain situations. He couldn't call a time-out in a pressure-packed NBA game with 6 seconds left and then begin to discuss which play to implement. These were already discussed.

Communication is key and how we approach the two-way conversations can make a huge difference. Timing is vital and these discussions are best at the end of the season, not during when emotions are high and athletes are competing. How you approach these conversations can make incredible strides towards being either a vicarious or supportive parent.

Co-author, Bill Parisi has worked with tens of thousands of athletes and parents. He contends asking soft questions is preferable to asking hard questions. Consider the one-on-one environment when having this discussion as well as a safe environment, such as over breakfast or lunch. Soft questions are non-confrontational and seek to understand experience. Hard questions are more focused on facts and knowledge than on understanding.

Delve deeper into understanding their perspective without becoming defensive. A hard question: "Isn't that why we paid for lessons?" A soft question: "Tell me about what you learned from this season?"

Hard questions also often turn into statements that attempt to fix the struggle: " we will need to talk to coach earlier." As opposed to soft questions that don't try to solve the problem. "Wow, that sounds like it was tough." A hard question creates an ultimatum about the immediate future: "Do you want to play sports?" A soft question addresses possibilities: "What do you think about taking some time off?"

Kids want to impress their coaches and parents. They want your approval! We must allow them an out, the emotional space to make their choices, and ensure that this is a path they want to continue.

It is important to know your child because one approach for a child may not work for another. The communication style can vary, and we must coach ourselves. The hardest thing to do for some parents is to not over communicate. It is having the same discipline as a parent that we want for our kids. If we expect our child to control their emotions and effort on the athletic field, then we need to prove we can control our emotions when mentoring them through sports and life.

The Gateway Drug to Specialization

Sport teaches what we want it to teach

—Jon Amaechi

National Baseball Director Keith Madison showed tongue-in-cheek that kids in the Dominican Republic exclusively play travel ball. They travel to the field by walking and they compete. No trophies at these games. He commented that these kids are "excited to get a bottle of water, and elated to get a used ball, cap or glove."

Traveling too early is the gateway drug to sports specialization. Kids should not participate in extended travel before late middle school. A few tournaments during the summer are great fun and important for experience, but today these showcases and tournaments are scheduled every single weekend. They are scheduled for exposure, not experience. Hanging over the head of parents is *if they want to play at the next level.* We applaud yet wince when parents have two kids in different sports around the same age. Their lives are centered and split between the sports and travel.

There is a cost of traveling too early. It becomes expensive once they start traveling, but the larger cost is a cognitive bias. It becomes too easy to buy the *idea* that they now have to pick one sport and stay with it.

Once dollars are shoveled into a sport too soon, it may be too late. Two seasons of early travel and you've invested a lot of money. The cognitive bias is that it can't go to waste and the kid *should* now stay involved at the highest level, which means year-round, early specialization to improve rapidly. This process occurring before age 13 or 14 means it is a huge risk of taking over the child's life.

Later on, traveling to a set number of showcases or large tournaments is wonderful. It is a great experience. However, we've seen the number explode to sometimes a dozen or more per year. Every large showcase or tournament does not need to be attended; make sure to limit the number attending. Have a plan in place of when and how much to travel and trust your plan.[40]

Parent Strategy: Take Time OFF

Robert Taylor Jr., owner of Smarter Team Training, is one of the best in the sports performance industry. He labels time-off for athletes as a time to "de-stress and decompress."

Parents often question why their son or daughter plays awful after five straight weekends on the road in the summer. Sophomores in college athletics ponder why they are tired all of the time. Simply put, never-ending competition does not allow for peak performance.

Competing is stressful. Training is tough. Winning and losing both take their toll on an athlete's psyche. There is now more attention surrounding everyone's record and statistics that it can add to the stress of poor play. Mix in some poor sleep habits, tough classes, and a rigorous training schedule, and there is a recipe for poor play. It may seem oversimplified, but so often overlooked: take some time off. Your child may not, so you need to be the one leading this effort to rest.

Quality sleep is paramount for good health and optimal performance. Too many people are going to bed late and getting up early as a badge of honor. Again, they wonder why they get sick? Under-sleeping is a curse in disguise because sleep repairs the mind and body, especially when we are young and in college. Lack of sleep is like working out and never taking time off.

Bring Back Sandlot

Creativity can be taught.

Professor Matt Bowers from the University of Texas examined the link between adult creativity and youth sport. His team assessed adult levels of creativity and youth sports experiences. Results were revealing.[41]

Time spent playing informal sports showed a positive and significant correlation with creativity. On the other hand, time devoted only to formal sports participation revealed a negative relationship with creativity. Organized sports hurt a child's creativity.

A recent IBM study of 1,500 CEO's showed that creativity was the primary "leadership competency" of the future. There is a creativity crisis. In society, intelligence scores have progressed upwards on a linear plane. Each generation shows scores increasing by 10 points. Creativity scores, however, have reversed and plummeted.

Early childhood development stresses free-play as the catalyst for creativity. Watch any young kids making forts, becoming Superman or pretending to be dinosaurs. Soon, free-play and creativity is no longer revered. Schools no longer have time for it, and video games at home have trumped free time.

The professionalization of youth sports has led to the elimination of unorganized, unstructured free-play (*Remember The Sandlot?*). Practice and play are parent-run. An adult viewpoint toward play is imposed on kids.

Sports have morphed into a mutated version where parents dictate, call the shots, and hand out the trophies. This doesn't draw the fun out of the sport; it merely sucks out the creativity. All kids have to do is show up and parents get the kids to buy in. The ownership is missing. Everything is structured for them. Kids are much more creative when given the freedom. There are no more bottle caps as the touchdown line or cars as the out of bounds. Fewer teams are being decided by shooting for sides.

It is also important not to surround our athletes with a constant cheering section and fan club. We develop best with no crowds, no one to play for, and no pats on the back. Athletes need a chance to figure things out for themselves, but instead coaches are doing all the thinking for them. Even open gym has become structured.

When young kids run the show, they figure it out on their own. Pick-up and street games are self-governed, self-policed, and encourage problem-solving. Kids take ownership. What develops is mental toughness—the willpower to fight, stand-up for oneself, and to find a way.

Head coach Andy Dorrel at Culver Academy pointed out that before the advent of text messaging, we actually had to walk over to the others to set up a game. Remember that? If no one was there, we were still outside. Another outside activity was bound to happen. Now, if no one answers the text, we are still on the couch.

The message is clear: Allow time for unstructured, unsupervised play. Encourage your kids to get together with friends or play with them. The off-season isn't meant to be spent on the couch—it is merely free from the pressure of competing in front of crowds. The problem solving and creativity they develop will last longer than any trophy from the league.

Injured—Now What?

Injuries change the way you approach the game.

—*Brett Favre*

Hall of fame athletic trainer Jenny Moshak worked alongside Pat Summit at the University of Tennessee for over 17 years. She treated injuries from nagging to the career-ending type. During one of her lectures she said, "An athlete who is injured goes through some depression."

She didn't mean clinical depression necessarily, although in some cases it's true. However, athletes go through feeling down, getting the blues, and can experience the negative thoughts and emotions that accompany depression.

Athletes deal with life through their sport and how they play. If they are playing well, a part of the team, and enjoying it, then all of life's problems fall into line. However, once an athlete becomes injured, every little problem becomes larger than life. Their coping mechanism has been removed and so they struggle and cannot deal. They may behave completely different, because their identity as an athlete is shaken.

Injuries are a catalyst for larger issues.

Often, athletes return to play too soon after an injury. They want to return and often will do whatever it takes. In the athlete's mind, they're feeling close to how they felt before the injury; however, after returning too fast, they soon discover they are off. They may feel fine for nine out of ten plays, but that one play where they can't cut, accelerate or move like before causes doubt.

Physically, it causes them to muscle guard and protect the injured area. Doubt, which has never been there before, is suddenly present. Doubt causes slight hesitations, over thinking or even trying to do too much. As a result of the doubt and less than stellar play, they lose confidence. It occurs at all levels and especially to the better players. Once an athlete loses confidence, it is extremely difficult to get it back.

Parent Strategy: The Injured Athlete

The role of the caregiver and coach is two-fold for injured athletes. First, ensure the athlete remains part of the team; stay included in travel, team functions, and especially practice. Second, stay in contact with the athlete and stay supportive, but relieve the pressure to return. Too often, injured athletes isolate themselves and start to internalize their struggle and don't reach out. Negative thoughts and feeling down can have a dramatic effect.

Sports Illustrated covered a story in 2015 involving injured athletes, however the authors addressed how the use of painkillers has transitioned into full-blown heroin abuse. Sadly, there is an epidemic in the United States involving prescription drug abuse and athletes are a sub-set.[42]

No athlete who gets injured says to themselves "I want to become an addict," their only goal at the time is to return to play. After a serious injury, they'll receive a prescription for an opioid painkiller such as Oxycontin, Percocet, or Vicodin. The athletes who take painkillers immediately become at-risk. Research revealed that high school male athletes are four times more likely to misuse painkillers than non-male athletes. The negative progression can spiral down fast because once their pills are no longer available an athlete will seek out other pills or cheaper means to maintain the painkiller high. The transition to heroin is actually fairly seamless since the molecular make-up of opioids is almost identical. They begin by smoking it and later injecting it.

Unfortunately, we've seen the progression. Prevention is key because there is no fast track or executive course to recovery. Opiate dependency is an on-going addiction that affects the entire family and community. Unfortunately if the community at large has an issue, it is safe to assume that the athletes themselves are part of it. You know your kids patterns so trust your gut when it comes to recognizing signs and behaviors. For example, do they complain about hurting but suddenly are no longer in pain? Has your own medicine cabinet been depleted? Are they sometimes sleeping in their same clothes? As advocate Marcus Amos states, "you can't prevent it, but you can prevent from participating in it." Further information on prescription dependency can be accessed through Centers for Disease Control and Prevention at www.cdc.gov.

Don't Should on Your Kids

Next Season

Life is not a dress rehearsal.

—Herm Edwards

At some point, all athletic careers end. It used to be the end of high school when this took place, but more recently, 85 percent drop out of sports by the age of 14. When they drop out from the sport so early, the long-term benefits haven't had a chance to take hold.

The saddest part, however, is that they simply stop playing. Think about it: How often in your life do you currently play? Hopefully, we do but often life gets in the way. They have their entire lives to grow up, but only one childhood to play and develop the love of playing. An adult viewpoint on youth athletics causes the fun to diminish and why would they pursue something that isn't really about having fun, but more about the external reward of playing at the next level?

This section is devoted to our IDENTITY—who are we and what our values, our real contributions are.

Who You I is Not Who You R

*What do you want to BE is different
than what do you want to DO.*

Curious why many high-profile athletes return to sport even after they retire? It's the same reason many professional athletes struggle with life issues when their career is over.

Elite athletes spend such a considerable amount of time on achieving their goals and these years include sacrifices both in and out of the sport. When they leave the sport, there is the immediate void that practicing and competition once filled. Being an athlete was their identity.

Then there are others who do not take on the athlete as their identity but rather, it is a role they are playing for a season in their life—something they do. These are the ones who successfully and easily transition out of the sport.

There is a huge difference between our identity and role. When we confuse these two, a struggle occurs. Athletes are the largest section of society that struggles with confusing one's identity with their roles. Our identity (I) is who we are, whereas our role (R) is what we do. Who you I is not who you R. Although important, the role of an athlete is just part of their identity. The family identity becomes wrapped up in the athletic success as well.

Dr. Mark Robinson's book *Athletic Identity* states that athletes not only play sports for the competition, but also for the entitlement and social aspect, including rewards, gifts, and social interactions. The entitlement factor shapes the athlete's world-view and their identity. When young athletes are treated like the cat's meow for their role, their identity can become skewed. And this is only the positive aspects we are considering in shaping our athletic role.[43]

We rarely look at how the negative features of being an athlete can affect our identity. For instance, specializing as a youth athlete closes off growth alternatives to one's identity. Johnny's identity as a star second-baseman is great until he is no longer the star second-baseman. Now he must struggle to find multiple identities, many which have been closed off because all he was known for is being a star second baseman. At some point, ceasing to play will occur for *every* athlete.

Social Media and Technology

The web has scaled everything down.

Kevin DeShazo, the founder of Fieldhouse Media, teaches social media best practices to collegiate and high school students. To illustrate the importance of social media, he tells a story that when Facebook was created, his first profile picture was actually of him picking his nose. And social media education is his profession.

Social media has completely changed the face of athletics, especially in the last ten years. Emojis, memes, GIF's, and vines, for example, have become part of the culture in just the past few years. Social media has scaled everything down so that what people were previously ignorant to is now widely known in a matter of minutes.[44]

Pat Welch won New Hampshire basketball player of the year. But after the state title game, which his team won, he lost the award. What never could have existed 10 years ago has changed the game. Pat made a poor decision: a bad tweet directed toward the team they had just beat. The tweet was only on-line for 15 minutes before he removed it however, the damage had been done. The basketball coaches retracted his award.[46]

On the positive side, a highlight film of an athletic performance shared on social media can delight millions of people in mere moments. On the flip side, an ill-advised post can now dampen a kid's future in a matter of seconds, with no way to take it back. It's amazing how much power each on-line post can have—and almost instantaneously—whether positive or negative. Once it is out there, it is influencing. College coaches follow possible recruits long before they can speak to them. Penn State assistant football coach Herb Hand tweeted out: *Dropped another prospect this AM due to his social media presence ... Glad I got to see the "real" person before we offered him.*[45]

This area of social media and technology is but one facet of how life has changed for our athletes. What is perhaps more important is the impact social media has created on our children's identity. Before, an athlete would have to search diligently for another player's talent level and performance. However, now, since the web has scaled everything down, comparison amongst athletes and parents is rampant. Comparison is the thief of all joy. The constant evaluation of others across many time zones can cause increased stress.

Your son or daughter will have a complete on-line profile before the time they are teenagers. Social media allows us to create a perception of how we want others to view us. To the average social media viewer, it would appear that everyone else is happy, beautiful, and successful leading the perfect life. We are often guilty of this misrepresentation too. How many of us post bad photos of ourselves?

If everyone else is perfect, and we are feeling sad or not good enough, this perception creates enhanced feelings of anxiety and perfectionism. Social media has exacerbated this level of comparison.

Madison Holleran was a beautiful, successful 19-year-old track athlete at the University of Pennsylvania. She was also a perfectionist who struggled with depression. Sadly, she took her own life during her freshman year. What is interesting about this occurrence is the role that she portrayed via social media. On Instagram, she would post pictures often that communicated the life she wanted others to see. Few could have been able to see the signs of a struggle.[47]

Social media has created another avenue to have difficult conversations. As parents, we are in charge of shaping our kid's identity and helping them differentiate it from their role.

Parent Strategy: Remove the Distraction

Communication is key to any successful relationship, whether it is between a player-coach, administrator-coach, spouse-spouse, or player-player. Sports like volleyball and basketball require constant communication. Teammates cannot text to one another on the court or field that they are open.

The volleyball team at Ohio Northern University had a strategy to increase communication among the team. They removed the biggest distraction to effective interactions. Before every road trip, every player put their phone in a basket for coaches to collect and the coaches returned their phones when they arrived back at campus. Some of us may cringe just thinking about giving up our phone.

The coaches realized that on the road trips, phones caused everyone to have their head down and in their own world, they would not talk with one another, they would text to their teammate behind them. The bus was often silent.

When coaches removed the phones, they talked with one another, joked around, and interacted. Communication improved. It made a vast difference not only off the court but on the court as well.

When the coaches returned the phones, it became a funny contest about how many hundreds of text messages each received. They also reverted quickly back the solo version of communication.

Phones and social media were an issue that coaches or parents 10 or more years ago did not have to encounter. Nonetheless, the coaches made an executive decision that was not popular at the time but was best for the team.

Scott McNealy, the father of top-ranked Stanford University golfer Maverick McNealy, placed specific guidelines on electronic device usage inside of the home. No phones or any electronics inside of the bedroom. The reasoning was that the bedroom was meant for sleeping and anything else was a distraction. Even studying was done outside of the bedroom.[48]

It was suggested to another parent seeking advice for his son's disrespectful behavior to remove his son's phone as a punishment. He dismissed the idea as foreign and exclaimed, "I could never do that!" This same father also refused to remove his son's activity of basketball. He viewed both as rights rather than privileges.

This is a more advanced time with more distractions than before. Technology has made most everything accessible and anonymous, which means free reign. As NFL coach Dick Vermeil stated, "Teams respond to discipline and attention to detail." We must not be afraid to make difficult decisions and set parameters about phones and electronics.

Our families should have guidelines in place of no phones at the dinner table. When you value the precious time that families spend together, phones simply interrupt.

Conclusion

Be the change you want to see in the world.

—GANDHI

In basketball, a popular move is the head fake, which gets the defender going one way while the dribbler goes the other way. So, here's the head fake. Hopefully, we think about how we can help our son or daughter with their mental toughness. But we need to start with ourselves. Our kids are not a reflection of our parenting, just a shadow.

We can't parent our kids to be more relaxed or mentally tough if we don't possess that quality. Our daughter won't listen to mom about her body image if mom doesn't value her body. If we are not patient or react badly when we lose our keys, then our kids will mirror this behavior. If we lose trust in others around us and blame and criticize, then our kids will serve as our shadow.

Being a supportive parent is difficult. Mental toughness is needed. It certainly hasn't gotten easier in today's culture, because there are so many more distractions. We are going to mess up and make mistakes. Remember, it's not about the setback; it's about the comeback. What's important is that we do the next right thing. When we do a poor job, own up to it. The key is to know that we can make adjustments and to show these adjustments. We can auto-correct when we notice that we've started talking about being nervous, discussing the game on the ride home, or putting more emphasis on winning rather than effort.

Our role as a parent is just part of our identity. It is a positive thing if we are not too wrapped up in our kid's lives. Some vicarious parents feel that their child's performance completely represents them. It can cause us as parents to stress out and lose perspective on the overall goal.

As we come to the close of this book, hopefully, you have gained a better understanding of how not to should on your kids. As you consider what you have just read, it is my hope you will have seen yourself in these words, or a vision of yourself you wish not to become.

Parenting Strategy: Ask the Right Questions

There is a saying—there's a good reason, and then there is the real reason. With that in mind, we want you to consider some of these important questions to ask yourself. Talk them over with your significant other. The way you answer these questions may give you a glimpse into whether you have been *shoulding* on your kid, and perhaps require an adjustment of direction.

- Why do you want your son or daughter to participate in sports?
- What do you want your child to become outside of sport?
- How much value do you place on academics?
- How often do we discuss winning and expectations as opposed to the effort?

The team that makes the fewest mistakes will win.

—GENERAL NEYLAND

The above is the first maxim created in the 1930's still used in football circles. Most games are lost more than they are won. This is true not only in sports and life but also in parenting.

There is not a one size fits all mentality to building mental toughness. Much of it depends on situations and experiences. For example, an injured athlete recovers better if they have been injured before because they cope with it better. We are going to make mistakes; that's not the goal. The objective is to become better ourselves so we can help our children become better.

One sharp word of criticism after a game or practice will do more harm than ten positive affirmations. It only takes one. We all can recall the incident when we felt shamed by a coach, family member or friend. There was so much emotion with the occurrence that it left a huge impression. With some of us, it became damaging.

Parenting out of anger or fear simply does not work. We need to be strategic and have a plan of helping our child build mental toughness. If our presence and feedback do not help our children, it will be difficult to handle, but that is the objective of not allowing it to be about us. It is sometimes better not to say anything than it is to make a mistake that loses the game.

Commend, don't criticize. Everyone has different shortcomings and weaknesses, and these are what cause us to lose games. Remember the goal.

References

1.	Popper, N. (2014, January 26). Committing to Play for a College, Then Starting 9th Grade. New York Times.

2.	Atkinson, J. (2014, May 4). How parents are ruining youth sports - The Boston Globe

3.	Valovich McLeod, T. C., Decoster, L. C., Loud, K. J., Micheli, L. J., Parker, J. T., Sandrey, M. A., & White, C. (2011). National Athletic Trainers' Association Position Statement: Prevention of Pediatric Overuse Injuries. *Journal of Athletic Training*, 46(2), 206–220

4.	Butler, S. (2011, April 29). $4,000 for Youth Baseball: Kids' Sports Costs Are Out of Control. *CBSNEWS*.

5.	Calonia, J. (2014, August 3). These Are the 5 Most Expensive Sports for Kids | GOBankingRates.

6.	Osterman, Z., & Neddenriep, K. (2014, April 25). Number of college basketball transfers escalating for various reasons. *Indy Star*.

6b.	Hoyt, E. (2015, February 3). New Trend: Parents Moving to College with Their Students. *Fastweb*.

7.	Karpf, R. (Director). (2013). *The Book of Manning* [Motion picture]. ESPN Home Entertainment.

8.	Frank, R. (2013, October 16). Spanx billionaire's secret to success: Failure. *CNBC*.

9.	Couric, K. (2009, Feb 8). Flight 1549: A Routine Takeoff Turns Ugly CBS: *60 Minutes*

10.	Akelson, M. (2010, May 9). Super Starks: The Story and Legacy of John Starks. *Bleacher Report*.

11.	Gibney, A. (Director). (2011). *Catching hell* [Motion picture]. ESPN Home Entertainment.

12.	Mello, I. (2015, January 30). Super Bowl 49: Not one starter was a 5-star recruit out of high school. *CBS Sports*.

13.	Peebles, M. (Director). (2011). *Herschel* [Motion picture]. ESPN Home Entertainment.

14.	Gould, D., Dieffenbach, K., & Moffett, A. (2002) Psychological Characteristics and Their Development in Olympic Champions, *Journal of Applied Sport Psychology*, 14:3, 172-204.

14b. Dell'antonia, K.J. (2015, September 8). Odds are, Your sport playing child isn't going pro. Now what? *The New York Times.*

15.   College Athletic Scholarship Limits - Scholarship Stats.com. (2013).

16.   Daniels, T. (2015, August 14). Cordell Broadus, Snoop Dogg's son gives up football. *Bleacher Report.*

17.   Holland, K & Schoen, J. (2014 October 14). Think athletic scholarships are the 'holy grail'? Think again. *ETNBC.com*

18.   Abrami, A. (2015, July 7). McRoberts leaves University of Vermont men's basketball. *Burlington Free Press.*

19.   Westham, A. (2014, February 27). Cardinal athletes weigh decisions to quit. *The Stanford Daily.*

20.   Tracking Transfer in Division I Men's Basketball. (2014, November 1). *NCAA.org*

21.   Nadeau, R. (2014, June 27). Size Matters: College Football's Biggest Offensive Linemen. *SportsNOLA.*

22.   Ringler, L. (2015, May 7). Deeper field, new format could create an NCAA postseason for the books. *GOLFWEEK.*

23.   Epstein, D. (2013). *The sports gene: Inside the science of extraordinary athletic performance.* London: Penguin Books

24.   Bell, R. (2012). *Mental Toughness Training for Golf.* Authorhouse.

25.   Miller, G. (1956). The magical number seven, plus or minus two: Some limits on our capacity for processing information. *Psychological Review* 63 (2): 81–97.

26.   (September 6, 2014). Stellar rookie performance overshadowed by Women's National Team's extra-inning loss. *Baseball Canada.*

27.   Pelham, B., Mirenberg, M., & Jones, J., (2002). Why Susie sells seashells by the seashore: Implicit egotism and major life decisions. *Journal of Personality and Social Psychology*, 82(4) 469-487.

28.   Bell, R. (2015). *NO FEAR: A Simple Guide to Mental Toughness.* DRB Press.

29.   Gregiore, C. (2015, April 1). Google makes you think you're smarter than you actually are. *The Huffington Post.*

30.   Wrzeniewski, A., & Schwartz, B. (2014, July 4). The Secret of Effective Motivation. *The New York Times.*

31.   Moor, B. (2015, May 17). Cheering Parents May Be Too Abundant. *South Bend Tribune.*

32. Markus, D. (1995, March 2). Smith put-back helps Maryland put down Duke. *The Baltimore Sun.*

33. ASAP Sports Transcripts (2015, June 4). NBA Finals- Cavaliers vs. Warriors Steve Kerr.

34. Shaw, J. (1995). How many bison originally populated western rangelands?. *Rangelands,* 148-150.

35. Loyola University Health System. (2013, April 19). Intense, specialized training in young athletes linked to serious overuse injuries. *ScienceDaily.*

36. Cook, B. (2015, May 8). What It Means To Youth Sports That Multi-Sport Athletes Dominated NFL Draft. *Forbes.*

37. Socci, B. (2013, December 5). IT HAPPENED TO ME: I Worked My Entire Life To Play Division I College Volleyball And Then Quit When I Got There. *Xojane.com*

38. Koba, M. (2014, January 13). Spending big on kids' sports? You're not alone. *CNBC.com*

39. Medic, N., Mack, D., Wilson, P., & Starkes, J. (2007). The Effects of Athletic Scholarships on Motivation in Sport. *Journal of Sport Behavior,* 30(3), 292-306.

40. Martinez, V. (2015, May 21). Being a great sports parent. *El Paso Times.*

41. Bowers, M., Green, B., Hemme, F., & Chalip, L. (2014). Assessing the Relationship Between Youth Sport Participation Settings and Creativity in Adulthood. *Creativity Research Journal,* 314-327.

42. Wertheim, J. L., & Rodriquez, K. (2015, June 22). Smack Epidemic: How painkillers are turning young athletes into heroin addicts. *Sports Illustrated.*

43. Robinson, M. (2014). *Athletic identity: Invincible and invisible, the personal development of the athlete.* First edition design publishing.

44. Patsko, S. (2015, February 3). How social media behavior of high school athletes can negatively impact NCAA recruiting: Photos, polls National Signing Day 2015.

45. Newport, K. (2014, March 28). New Hampshire HS Basketball player of the year loses award after obscene tweet. *Bleacher Report.*

46. Boren, C. (2014, July 30). Penn State assistant says football recruit was dropped over 'social media presence.' *The Washington Post.*

47. Fagan, K. (2015, May 7). Split Image. *ESPNW.*

48. Newport, J. (2015, May 8). The Golf Upstart of Silicon Valley. *The Wall Street Journal.*

Don't Should on Your Kids